Fatherless Women

Fatherless Women

How We Change After We Lose Our Dads

Clea Simon

John Wiley & Sons, Inc.

New York • Chichester • Weinheim • Brisbane • Singapore • Toronto

No part of this publication may be reproduced, stored in a retrieval system, or transmitted in any form or by any means, electronic, mechanical, photocopying, recording, scanning, or otherwise, except as permitted under Section 107 or 108 of the 1976 United States Copyright Act, without either the prior written permission of the Publisher, or authorization through payment of the appropriate per-copy fee to the Copyright Clearance Center, 222 Rosewood Drive, Danvers, MA 01923, (978) 750-8400, fax (978) 750-4744. Requests to the Publisher for permission should be addressed to the Permissions Department, John Wiley & Sons, Inc., 605 Third Avenue, New York, NY 10158-0012, (212) 850-6011, fax (212) 850-6008, e-mail: PERMREQ@WILEY.COM.

This publication is designed to provide accurate and authoritative information in regard to the subject matter covered. It is sold with the understanding that the publisher is not engaged in rendering professional services. If professional advice or other expert assistance is required, the services of a competent professional person should be sought.

Portions of this book were previously published in a different form in *The Boston Globe*.

Library of Congress Cataloging-in-Publication Data is available from the publisher.

ISBN 0-471-41006-3 (cloth : alk. paper)

Printed in the United States of America

10 9 8 7 6 5 4 3 2 1

For Jon, for my mother, Iris,
and in memory of my father, Eugene Protter Simon

Contents

Introduction

Writing about my father is about as easy as wading through wet cement. My father, who died nearly eight years ago as I write this, was a complicated man, and my relationship with him was equally complex. A self-professed intellectual, an Ivy League-educated doctor, and enthusiastic supporter of the arts, he took pride as much in the differences between himself and others of his class as in his achievements. Unlike many of his medical colleagues, he claimed to dislike the barriers of status that separated the doctor from the patient, and (particularly in a suburb like ours, with its underpinnings of immigrant, small-town feudalism) from the community at large. Unlike many of his peers in education, those who sat next to him at the opera and the symphony, he was proud of his appreciation of popular culture, particularly any tunes he thought resembled those of the Beatles. Unlike many other men of his era—he was forty years old when I, his youngest child, was born—he believed he had remained current in his thoughts and views. Except, of course, where his youngest child, his second daughter, was concerned.

He was a complex man, despite his affability and the great joy he took in simple pleasures—good food, a long walk on a fine day. And to write about him, particularly to write about my relationship with him, brings back all the convolutions, all the contradictions, that I couldn't reconcile during his life. Wading through them now, when some of the issues, at any rate, seem to have been resolved, cannot be a straightforward journey. This father-daughter relationship was sometimes tortured, often peaceful and full of love. To go back and view our interactions with honesty requires a kind of double-tracking memory. It calls for the ability to see how I wished (and sometimes believed) we were then, and also to see the way we were truly interacting, with all the currents and sub-currents of fears and expectations that dragged at us both. Writing about my father, about being my father's daughter, means reviving decades-old feelings of confusion and anger, of insecurities that reached so deep that I did not know how to trust myself with this life. Writing about my father, about our relationship, means writing about everything I would rather not face.

How could it not? I was my father's baby, a "daddy's girl" in many ways. I was his favorite of his three children for a number of reasons, including my resilient mental health, which was apparent early on in stark contrast to the schizophrenia that enveloped both my older siblings as they went through puberty, and which con-fused and hurt him by its refusal to respond to treatment, to rea-son, or to the force of his will. I was, by virtue of my health as well as by birth order, his hope for the future and his ally. But because he had seen my brother and my sister falter and stumble, and because he was in many respects a patriarch in the Old World mold, I was also his hostage, the one he was going to carry suc-cessfully through life, her protests notwithstanding.

In short, because of the accidents of our family, and because of who he was, I don't know if he ever tried to understand who I was, or who I was capable of becoming, as I progressed from his preco-cious little bookworm to a rebellious teen and then a young woman. For I spent much of my time while he was alive respond-ing to his cues, which often meant yielding my will to his. And while he believed that he was open to the world, I see now that by the time I was born, he had in many ways closed himself into a small, tight circle of beliefs that ultimately excluded much of what my life, as an adult woman, has come to be about. Writing about him, therefore, is often painful, as each good memory either brings forth a bad one, or is followed swiftly by the saccharine aftertaste that lets me know that once again, as I did so often in my childhood, I am avoiding the unpleasant, the unhappy, and the true.

To write about my father, therefore, is once more to interact with him, and that brings up all the unresolved issues and personal contradictions I bring to our relationship. Trying to decipher the influence of my father, of his legacy, I am once more a little girl, dependent and trusting and sometimes betrayed. I am again an adolescent, angry and more vulnerable than I seem. Although many pop psych books want to freeze our relationships with our fathers into specific categories, to make us the "eternal girl" or the "stubborn teen" in all our dealings, the truth is more fluid. On any given day, and in every interaction, I am all the female roles, and he is all the male ones, and I do not think that I am unique in this way. Anything less, any kind of simplification of our dance, leads to error.

Only one truth appears simple, one set of facts that help anchor me. With all the pain and hesitation that I felt—that I still feel—about my father, about his illusions and his intelligence, his child-like and openhanded generosity and the harsh and unappealable judgments he could bring down, I am only sure of this: He was my father and he is dead. And now that his active presence in my life is through, I can begin to see him as a complete and separate entity. I can begin to understand his continuing effect on me. For despite his no longer being a commonplace presence in my life, this complex and contradictory man is very much a part of me. No matter how I approach the subject, I am still my father's daughter. And no matter how much my life has changed since his passing, he is influencing me. By example, by comparison, by his shadow, and by the passing of that shadow, my father remains very present in my life.

The inspiration for this book came from a series of changes that I noticed in my life after my father died, then witnessed again in the lives of friends as they also lost their fathers. These changes appeared small at first, but what I saw was that within a few years of our bereavements, their cumulative effect was overwhelming. Five years down the line, a great number of us had changed careers or the style of work we did. We had been stubbornly single, and then we married, or we had been unhappily anchored and were finally able to leave relationships that we had outgrown. We found ourselves free to drop decades-old obsessions, to let gripes and worries finally be. Beyond the very real but temporary dislocation of grief, we seem to have changed, to have learned from our losses. Despite our pain, we seem for the most part to have gotten stronger. And although these changes may be seen as the kind of growing that we women in our thirties and our forties would have done anyway, the nature of these shifts, and the fact that many of us had been unable to make them earlier, suggests a connection between our losses and our gains.

To be realistic, these changes are what therapists would call overdetermined. They are decided by multiple factors—our age and our experience as well as the death of our male parents—and no one influence can explain all our growth. But over all of the changes we've experienced hangs the shadow of our fathers, or perhaps the sudden absence of that shadow, an experience I've confirmed with dozens of women and with psychiatric professionals who work with families and with women going through transitions. Keeping in mind that many elements contribute to every stage in our lives, I became interested in the father factor—in how the loss of our paternal parents in some way altered us, either freed us to act or spurred us to make moves in our own lives, and in how their presence had influenced both who we had been and who we were now able to become.

I have begun by examining my own life in terms of the shifts I observed first in my work, then in my internal landscape, and finally in the composition of my friendships and intimate relationships over the first few years after my father's death. None, to state the obvious, was done consciously, or rather, all were the kinds of transformation I had wished for, but had been unable to achieve in the first thirty-one years of my life. Simply put, despite years of therapy and hard thinking about my life, I had had no idea, while my father was alive, how to make these leaps in growth and love. Then, suddenly, I was making them. Something beyond willpower and ambition was at work; some energy that had been tied up in some way with my father was now set free.

The first change I noticed in my own life was very basic. I attributed it at the time to the stress of that winter, the months of watching my father decline and the weeks of visiting at the hospital where he finally succumbed to the cancer that had begun in his prostate and then infiltrated his bones. For what happened that winter, even as he became sicker and more frail, growing increasingly irascible and peevish with his weakness and his pain, was that I became more honest, stronger at facing what I did not like. The way that I witnessed this, through fatigue that blessedly kept my guilt at this growth at bay, was that my work as a journalist and essayist was getting better, my writing less constrained.

As miserable as I felt, this was meager compensation, but I grabbed at it. That winter, as he declined into an uneasy death, the stories I wrote—occasionally about him—became more clear-sighted and less sentimental. The topics that appealed to me were more immediate, my style cleaner and more concise. I told myself at the time that I was worn out, that the exhausting weight of anticipatory grief had made me less tolerant of journalism's conventions and its ridiculous expectations of distance and objectivity, that I simply had lost the touch for lightness and fancy in my writing, and perhaps in my life. And I hoped—for even then I realized that I had made a qualitative leap in my work—that the change would be permanent. I wanted to have been tried in the fire of the horrible experience that was my father's slow dying and come out somehow purified. I wanted his death to mean something, to have served in this way as a gift to me. Perhaps for a while I even believed this was true.

But the second change I noticed served to disprove this ennobling myth, or at least recast it in ways that I hadn't contemplated. For the second change I noticed in myself through the rest of that long, miserable winter was not an unalloyed benefit. It was not particularly complimentary to my father or myself, nor were its benefits immediately obvious. What I first thought, when I noticed a change (as if I were standing outside myself and watching myself run along a strange new set of tracks) was that I seemed to have lost the gift for connection. Throughout that winter and into the spring of my father's death, I saw myself cool, as if my sense of intimacy and vulnerability was undergoing a chemical transformation. I thought I had become heartless. Whereas before I had been a bonding molecule, drawn to others and to whom others attached, afterward I seemed to have had my ions reversed, so that instead of attaching, I recoiled, bouncing from contact to contact without ever changing or being changed.

This makes me sound promiscuous, and I was not, no more than any of my single female friends. But before my father's final illness I had always put a premium on relationships, on making an emotional connection no matter how inappropriate or unlikely to last. In the months before my father's death, in fact, I had only with difficulty ended a long-term relationship that had turned sour soon after its start—two years with a man who epitomized my father's brilliance and desire for control without any of his sense of propriety or kindness. And only a month before my father was hospitalized for the final time, I had been shattered by the collapse of a shorter pairing, a rebound affair certainly, but one that seemed at the time to hold promise of something more. In the weeks following my father's hospitalization, however, I found that something had changed in me, in my attitude toward the men I met and dated and slept with, toward my own physical reaction. I found myself, in the middle of an evening with a very handsome co-worker, quite bored. *He's not that smart*, I remember telling myself. *But he is awfully pretty.* I took him home that night because I wanted to, and thought little about it the next day. The old stirrings were there—*wouldn't it be great if we could fall in love? wouldn't that be wonderful?*—but a new clear-eyed, colder self was emerging.

Wouldn't it be great if pigs had wings? I remember laughing at myself, at the vestiges of regret, as I changed the sheets. It was as if the softness in me had been sloughed off as of no more use than a lizard's tired skin. Ultimately, what would be left would be, like my writing, more muscular and more honest. Although that winter found me disconnected, for that wasn't the only incident, I now believe my heart was simply shifting its priorities, realigning to reality, and readying for the kind of deeper commitments that had eluded me before.

These changes were, I now believe, related. Affecting both my work and my attitude toward the men with whom I became involved, these were signs of growth the full implications of which I wouldn't recognize for years. Perhaps at thirty-one I was finally ready for a new life, for the more serious attitude these changes implied. But in retrospect, I see the loss of my father as a crucial factor in this growth, in my ability to finally walk away from childish ways that no longer served me or my family. Although other factors certainly played a part, one is certain: I had lost my father, and in him I had lost the fantasy of Daddy, of the one man who was going to take care of me. The one man who clearly *had* to care for me, the corollary being that he had to because I could not care for myself. But in giving up that fantasy, I was also abandoning the image I had of myself as a woman who needed to be taken care of. I was losing, at a disconcerting rate, my illusions.

I recall feeling a little embarrassed in my new skin, the kind of slight shame one has when one discovers that one has been walking around with a seam open at the back or an undergarment peeking out. Had I been that helpless, that girlish for this long? Had I really allowed myself to be infantilized in that many critical areas?

Mercifully, that's when I began to realize that many other women I knew were undergoing the same kinds of transformations. Rona, single for years, started dating a truly nice man. Lita did the same, and soon after announced her intention of leaving the law, a profession she had always expressed ambivalence about although it was one her father revered. Ellen bought a house and decided to adopt a child. Kendra quit fretting about her position as a proofreader, a job her father had derided, and learned to enjoy the companionship her office life offered. Cara told me about the happy second marriage that had followed the loss of her father, and from Irina and Rikki, Nora and Tracy I heard a range of reactions, all life-changing, that had filled the approximately eighteen months following their fathers' deaths. In our work, in our living situations, in our relationships with family members as well as with significant others we were reacting to our fathers' deaths with emotional leaps that in their breadth surprised us. We were suddenly, in our grief and mourning, growing up.

There have been many studies of inappropriate relationships and of women who find themselves trapped in outgrown patterns, particularly with their male parents. The best of these, such as Linda Schierse Leonard's *The Wounded Woman*, convey that although we may be caught up in immature patterns of behavior that do not best serve our needs as independent adults, we need not consider ourselves entirely to blame nor be completely blocked by these outdated behaviors. Leonard understands that the situations are complex, that we may derive lasting benefits from our inappropriately girlish or scared or defiant behavior, and that such internalized roles are to be understood, forgiven, and incorporated into the majority of our lives. Most of these books, even the more dated—such as *Fathers and Daughters*, by the Harvard-affiliated psychiatrist William S. Appleton, which once may have been held up as the standard for this field of study, or Suzanne Fields' popular-psychology *Like Father, Like Daughter*—pay lip service to the concept that we may embody several such types during our lives. Although they tend to simplify to the point of error, even they detail how and why we may act out different roles at different times and under different stimuli. I name these books as a way of suggesting them, with caution, as works that helped me understand the factors that led to the changes in my own life and in the women around me.

I have also talked to more than a hundred women. I have interviewed in person and by telephone more than seventy volunteers, and read the first-person accounts of as many again. There are women I found through personal contacts, the friends of friends and sisters of colleagues, as well as through ads on web sites and in such publications as Wellesley College's *Women's Review of Books* and local newspapers. These volunteers agreed to fill out a questionnaire that grew and changed as I learned more from the responses I received. To encourage candor, I have changed all these women's names to pseudonyms, and many identifying details have been altered to further ensure anonymity and privacy. In addition, I've mined the existing literature, from fictional references in novels like Melissa Bank's *The Girl's Guide to Hunting and Fishing* and Anna Maxted's *Getting Over It*, and in the many memoirs, essays, and poems dealing with both grief and growth to understand the complex individuality of our reactions and also to find the themes and behaviors common to women in transition.

We are not all alike. I have met women who went through mourning but whose lives did not change. There were women whose marriages survived intact or whose dating patterns never faltered, and those whose careers and thoughts on children and the future remained stable and consistent even years after this life-changing event. But they were in the minority, and I could not say with certainty that these women as a whole were either necessarily healthier or more entrenched in the past than those of us who found our lives turned upside down. I realize that to some extent my subjects—the women who agreed to talk and to write to me of their deepest, most personal experiences—are what a formal scientist would dismiss as a self-selected group; a population, in other words, that already had a vested interest in my questions and my conclusions and was not, perhaps, an accurate sample of all women who have lost their fathers. I have no way of correcting for this flaw, although by acknowledging it I hope to bring it to the attention of the reader. And I do not think it invalidates the truths that I have uncovered. I have spoken to enough women from all over the country, from various fields and faiths and stages of life, to convince me that despite the disparities that make all our lives unique, there truly is something like a shared experience for many of us here. That for many of us, somehow, the loss of our fathers triggered changes and brought about a time of growth that helped us realize fullness in our lives. I have realized that our fathers' true impact upon us often could not be felt without their absence. That we could not see who we were, as their daughters and as the grown women we had become, until they were gone.

Partly because I am following my own experience, and partly because this is an informal, intuitive study, I am not dealing here with the effects of abusive relationships. There is much to be said about such painful relationships, about the scars of incest and the wounds of neglect, shame, pain, and fear. On occasion such factors did surface among the women with whom I spoke, but although I want to allow these women their voices, I am not focusing on the aftereffects of these particularly and horribly damaging father-daughter relationships. I am dealing here with women who may have had imperfect relationships with their fathers, who may in fact have been damaged and hurt, but who on the whole define their childhoods as more or less normal. We are women whose fathers may have let us down as often as they buoyed us up, who scared and disappointed us when we needed their hugs and encouragement, and with whom we had conflicts both open and unstated. But still we believed ourselves loved by them; they were men we trusted, on whom we could usually rely. There are fine books and many still to be written about blatantly unhealthy relationships; my concern is with the more commonplace ones, the father-daughter relationships we recognize around us every day.

To do this, I have realized, I have had to delve into two separate areas. I have had to look at how we mourn and recover from the loss of a parent and also how we, as adult daughters at this point in history, were raised by our fathers. It's a complicated intersection, the meeting of grief and growing, and at first glance the subjects seem so unrelated as to be impossible to match up, as if we were making an apples-and-oranges pie and couldn't figure out how to get the filling to set. All I had to go on was the instinct that there was such an intersection, and that it played a crucial role in my life and in the lives of women like me.

Clearly, my book could not do both of these broader subjects justice in any kind of quantitative or scientific sense. And although much fine writing has been done on grief (notably by Elisabeth Kubler-Ross, Edward Myers, Lily Pincus, and Lois Akner, whose works I drew on for this book), and on the development of young women and the influence of their fathers (such as the excellent studies by Carol Gilligan, Michael Lamb, Henry Biller, Patricia Reis, and others), this is not such a book. I am, instead, trying to fix a point in time, a moment when things change and from which there is no turning back, and by looking at that moment—at the event that will occur to more than half the women in this country before they are fifty years old—I am trying to understand what happens next, in terms of our lives, in terms of our pasts as our fathers' daughters, and in terms of who we will be in our new lives, after our fathers have gone.

Fatherless Women

CHAPTER 1

After Daddy

Speaker wire doesn't usually faze me. A music fan since childhood, I'd run the plastic-coated copper down dorm halls and up stairwells and in a dozen empty rooms. I knew how to strip the ends, and twirl the wire inside to a fine solid contact. But six years ago, faced with a mop bucket of shiny coils, of plug-in connectors and double-headed inputs, I found myself giving in to that deep fatigue that, for me, is the final embodiment of grief. You see, the last time I had tried to set up my stereo, my father had been there to help me.

The last time I had moved, about five years earlier, my parents had recently retired, relocating from our big family house several hours away to a nearby condo. And I had just gone through one of those crushing breakups that always seemed to outweigh whatever good the original relationship had held. My father had time on his hands, I was temporarily incapacitated, and so he had come over with his wire cutter and staple gun and taken over the installation of my stereo system. He had hooked up the tape deck and turntable, arranged the speakers for maximal stereo separation, and then worked his way down my new apartment's long hallway, tracing molding and doorways and neatly affixing the wires out of sight so that my back room would have the same sound options as the front of the narrow flat. I'm not sure how much his work that day went toward soothing my broken heart, but I know that every time I noticed his handiwork—when I finally replaced the turntable with a CD player, when I upgraded those back-room speakers—I felt his presence. My father had taken care of me. He had been there to worry about the details.

And then he was gone, victim of a three-year-long battle with prostate cancer that left him shrunken and angry, and robbed him of his jovial can-do attitude long before it took his life. And although I had mourned him at his death and kept my loss in the front of my mind for months after, the stupid ache of grief kept sneaking up on me regularly, draining me of my energy. By the time I had finally ripped up those neat double tracks of wire, I had thought I was past the worst of it. Then something like this, a bucket of speaker wire, would set me off. My father wasn't going to take care of me anymore. My daddy was gone.

I don't recall how long I sat there, boneless, breathless, staring at that bucket of wire, or even if I got around to the task that day. But I do know that before the week was out either I, or the boyfriend with whom I had rented the apartment, had laid that wire out, had connected the speakers, the tape deck, and the CD player. Even the old turntable was fixed into the system, ready to play the boxes of vinyl that neither of us had the heart to replace. And somewhere in there it began to dawn on me: My father was gone, and I sorely missed him, but I was doing okay. More than okay, actually. The apartment I was setting up was the first I had shared with a man, the first time in my thirty-three years that I felt secure enough in a relationship to begin to build a home with someone. The speaker wire might not be as neatly laid down as if my father had done it, but the apartment was comfortable, big and airy. And I needed the music system to be hooked up because I was settling down to write my first book, the kind of project I had long dreamed of tackling. No matter which angle I looked at my life from, it seemed I had grown up a lot in the two years since his death, from pampered daughter to self-sufficient adult. I remembered a retort he had once snapped at me, overcome by what he saw as my naivete when dealing with an abusive boss: "When are you going to stop being such a good girl," he'd asked me, "and start being a smart woman?" Maybe it had taken his death to free me to do just that.

Our Fathers' Roles

In so many ways, we measure ourselves by our fathers, especially once they are gone. "He was very proud of me, but we never got along," one woman tells me, recalling the distant, stubborn man who died three years before. "We were really similar—very, very stubborn and very opinionated. We butted heads on everything."

"We didn't go in for conflict in my family. Avoidance was the way to deal with stuff," explains another. "He couldn't stand it when I cried when I was angry or upset, and all my life he would say sharply, 'Stop crying!' And that of course just made me angrier and more upset." These conflicts and contests stay with us, so that even when the opposing voice is silenced we hear the words, the angry or critical or sometimes adoring tone in our heads, and we continue to respond.

What happens to us when we lose our fathers? This is a question that most of us will have to answer in our lifetime; U.S. Census figures report that by the age of fifty more than half of us will have outlived our fathers, twice as many as will have outlived our mothers. More than a quarter of us will be adults before this loss, and that blurs our issues, mutes in some ways our reactions to the deaths of the men who have been our parents. Long before our fathers die, for example, we will no longer be looking to them to fulfill the traditional role of parents, to feed or clothe us, shelter or protect us, as we had as children. Ideally, many of us will have grown past the conflicts that led us to defy them or that challenged us to grow and thrive despite them. We no longer fear our fathers, or worship them as gods, at least not consciously. But for most of us our fathers continued to loom large in our lives. No matter how close to or distant from our fathers we were at the time of their deaths, they were important to us. Their loss changes our personal cosmography. Our worlds are no longer warmed by the same sun or shadowed by the same dark planet; however they exerted their force, the gravity that pulled at us has shifted.

One liberty that their loss has bought for us is the freedom to look, for the first time perhaps, at who our fathers were, and at what they meant to us. As simple as this sounds, there has not been much examination of this relationship in traditional psychology. What research there is primarily concerns itself with child development, and usually looks at mothers' influences or at parental interaction with children of either gender. Very little formal work examines the lifelong impact of a father on his female children.

Study of fathers and daughters got off to a rocky start. Freud virtually abandoned the study of fathers' effects on their girl children when, confused and apparently repelled by his female patients' tales of incest and sexual encounters, he rejected what these women were telling him. Although he twisted these revelations into the "penis envy" theory, he did finally acknowledge that his own explanation was flawed. Still, his inexact and frightened work has been taken as the basis for much subsequent theorizing, most of it built around our supposedly unresolved Oedipal (or, for our gender, Elektra) complexes, which have us still wanting to seduce Daddy as a major goal in life. More recently, feminist theorists and psychoanalysts, such as Jessica Benjamin and Nancy Chodorow, have tried to distinguish between the gender of our parents and the roles they played, showing how, for example, it was not our fathers' penises that we wanted for ourselves as much as their independent lives.

Even in theories of family dynamics, fathers have gotten short shrift. Most works on bonds and influences (such as the theory of attachment championed by John Bowlby) consider fathers distinctly less important than mothers as active, involved parents, especially in relation to their female children. More contemporary researchers, such as Henry B. Biller and Michael Lamb, have spent the last few decades catching us up on the role of the father in the family, particularly in the education of infants and young children. Both, however, have focused more on general child-raising, without distinguishing much between daughters and sons, and neither have dwelt on lifelong effects. As a result, we must reexamine the basics. We must decipher, for example, how our fathers differed from our mothers in terms of their roles in our lives and their influences on our behavior.

Some of these distinctions are obvious and can be found in traditional psychological literature. Shedding the sexist language that clouds much of this early work, the theory is simple: While our mothers often melded with us—their children and especially their like-gendered girl children—our fathers usually represented some form of opposition. Disciplinarian or taskmaster, doting daddy or indulgent sweetheart; in some ways, most family therapists and theorists agree, our fathers were the first *others* in our lives, the first people who were clearly *not* a part of who we were in the same intrinsic way that our mothers so definitely were. They stood apart from us. We saw ourselves in their eyes, and defined ourselves by who they were, who they wanted us to be, and who we wanted them to be. Unlike our mothers, they were clearly separate from us. We grew up, in part, learning to define our own independence against them. When they are gone, we are forced to look for new rules, new standards against which to measure our freedom, our accomplishments, and our goals.

With this freedom comes a new clarity of vision, an ability to see the fathers that we have lost. Often the first things we see, once our grief has lessened, are the specific details that separated us. The differences between who we wanted them to be and who they actually were. Irascible, stubborn, and sometimes bullying, or weak, overly sensitive, and somehow flawed, they were our dads. Whatever degree of adult objectivity or maturity we had achieved while our fathers were living, we may find magnified. This is our opportunity to view our fathers as multifaceted, as people who played out different roles in different contexts, as husbands to our mothers, as sons to their parents, as men in the adult world, as well as fathers to us.

Sometimes what we see surprises us. We may, for example, suddenly recognize the pressures that made our fathers overly strict or simply overtired. Conversely, we may for the first time perceive flaws and faults that in retrospect explain undercurrents that we never understood.

"To be frank, I'm learning he was a great dad and a not-so-great husband," one woman says to me. "Since his death I'm less likely to see him as either a victim or a villain and better able to understand him as a complicated person," adds another as soon as we begin to talk. In short, once they are gone we begin to see them as people, just like us.

These days I can look back on my father's towering rages and wonder how I ever reconciled these with the utterly benign image of the "good daddy" that I clung to into adulthood. While he was living, I never could seem to recall him acting frustrated, only kind, generous but not mean-spirited, and I dismissed all the evidence of my senses, all memory, to the contrary. He was my father, the closest thing to a family god I ever was to know. And while some theorists will point to this failing as a flaw in my own stumbling climb to adulthood, I'm not sure how it could have been much different. To be sure, some women learn to see their parents truly, warts and all, while they are still alive. But our fathers carry so much weight in our lives, they have so thoroughly taught us fear if not respect, that many of us are unable to make this perceptual leap while they are alive. After talking to so many women, I no longer trust the self-help books that would have us believe that it is the rare woman who recedes into girlhood awe or passivity around her father. I believe nearly all of us do, at some place in our hearts, and that not until our fathers are permanently, finally removed from us do we get the opportunity to step beyond what Australian author Carmel Bird calls "their long shadows" and see the men who have been towering over us.

New Freedoms

I know that my image of my father has grown in complexity since he died. With his death, I have seen not only my own contradictory illusions, but also the human motives that can reconcile what I remember. In my case, I have begun to see a man who believed strongly in a particular code of ethics, a strict set of behaviors, which kept him on a particular track for good and ill throughout our family's many misadventures. This must have been sorely tested, for example, when two of his children developed serious mental illnesses and his one son killed himself, but my father held to his principles. He kept what was left of the family together, he stayed with his grieving wife, and supported his surviving children as best he could. No wonder his patience sometimes wore thin with me, as the usual scrapes of childhood and adolescence grated on his stoic demeanor. No wonder he sometimes flared up for what at the time seemed like no reason. I no longer remember him as the perfect dad, the wonderful bringer of treats. But perhaps I better understand why.

This ability to see him in full, however, has come to me only in his absence and only with time, as my need and nostalgia for the false image of him fades. And as he becomes clearer to me in memory, so too does his influence over me. Indeed, this is the second focus of the increasing clarity of vision that I am learning is common among those of us who survive our fathers. For me, it is a mixed vision. Looking back, I can begin to make out how he helped me grow in ways that continue beyond his lifespan. I can also see also how he forced me into stagnation, out of fear or out of hope of an impossible outcome, tying me to a standard in which I did not myself believe. He was such a big figure in my life that only now, eight years after his death, can I begin to see who I am beyond his shadow, what I am "after Daddy."

Psychologists and sociologists have been aware of the general impact of parental death on adult children for decades. In general, their studies have focused on the death of both parents, and the realization, by the adult, that she or he is no longer anyone's child. Along with the grieving and the reevaluating of familial roles that occur, for many this orphaning serves as a great impetus to action, and to growth. "The loss of a parent rouses the need to progress, to mature, to be potent," writes Lily Pincus in *Death and the Family*. "The death of a parent can be a catalyst for important changes," reiterates Lois Akner in *How to Survive the Loss of a Parent*. Author and journalist Victoria Secunda has written a book concisely titled *Losing Your Parents, Finding Your Self*.

Some of those general changes encountered by the adult who loses a parent may be understood in the light of theories of personality development. The psychoanalyst Carl Jung, for example, talked about our separation from our parents (the process he named individuation) as the means by which we learn that we are our own people, capable of setting our goals and boundaries. This process, ideally, lasts throughout our early adulthood and may be complete by middle age. Otto Rank, who followed up on Jung's work, believed that most people do not complete this process and instead remain stuck in the first step, at which we accept our parents' and our society's goals and ideals as our own. Many psychologists and psychoanalysts since have discussed ways of finalizing the process, usually through the self-examination of therapy, during which we can explore and finally untangle the knots that have held us back. But for many of us, the shock of death may serve as a powerful impetus—what psychologist Patricia Reis calls a "motivating disaster"—that jars us out of complacency and allows us a rare chance to look at ourselves in a fresh light.

For daughters who have lost their fathers, that new view can be startling and even freeing. Consider the specific roles that fathers have played in our lives, and we can see the range of changes that suddenly become possible. Our work lives and sense of self-esteem are freed from decades-old ghosts. Our feelings about the families we have formed in adulthood, through ties of love and birth, and feelings about our families of origin may be sifted and sorted out in ways we never before thought possible. We may be freed from duties that have not been appropriate since adolescence. We may find ourselves dropping outlived rebellions and rediscovering long-buried parts of ourselves. We may find ourselves newly able to open up to others.

Indeed, it is in our most intimate relationships that these changes may be most deeply felt. Our fathers loomed so large in our lives, after all, that they often left little room in our hearts and minds for other romantic partners. Not that our closeness to our fathers was unhealthy in the expected dramatic ways; for the vast majority of women I've spoken with, incest was not an issue, although its vaguer emotional counterparts—a father's inappropriate interest in our appearance, or overly possessive attachment to us—may have been. But the emotional heft of our relationships with our fathers often weighed us down. Many of us spent so much time looking for men like our dads—or avoiding those who at all resembled them—that we had difficulty finding men who could meet the needs of who we actually were, of the grown women we had become.

My story is not the only one. Rona, for example, could not settle down as a grown woman in a relationship of her own until the loss of her father. For Rona, as for many women like her, romance had always been difficult, relationships with men short-lived. Now easing into her mid-forties, she had grown up knowing her father doted on her, convinced that he found her lovable. If anything, he was overly involved in her life. He was never inappropriate, but in a thousand small, intrusive ways he made sure he was the focus of her life, that he was necessary to her happiness, if not her survival.

Her memories of him are fond. She laughingly describes him as a "Jewish mother" type who always asked if she had eaten, always checked to make sure his "girl" was all right. He never said he wanted to be the center of her life, but while he was around she was unable to let any other man in. Now, after a five-year dry spell, she finds herself involved with a man. Although they have just begun to talk about moving in together, she notes that this relationship already has a different feel to it. And she wonders how much her father's presence, well-intentioned as it was, had kept her from the love she sought.

"I've found that his death has helped me be more open about emotions," she says. "This emotional growth has helped in my ability to start the relationship I seem to be in now. In a weird way, it's been freeing. Not so much knowing that my father's not here to take care of me as just understanding the role he played in my family, and in my life."

Reevaluating Our Lives

The ripple effect of our loss reaches every aspect of our lives. Women who had already established stable, lasting relationships talk of experiencing a power shift, a flip between their partners and parents, or between themselves and their partners. Such shifts, when they happen, may be immediately apparent and then fade away within a year or even two, the balance corrected. Sometimes the changes that come about may be longer-lasting. Rikki, a social worker and the mother of three boys, tells me about separating from her husband after her father's death. Losing her father, she explains, started her thinking about the power plays that had ruled her parents' marriage, and this led her to examine the interactions in her own. Once her father's powerful presence no longer towered over her and her mother's life, she could clearly see how she had unconsciously adopted patterns and beliefs from their marriage, relics that didn't fit her image of herself as an adult. She and her husband have since reconciled and had a fourth child, their daughter, through a decision that they reached together. But for Rikki marriage—and her own assumptions—will never be the same. "I'm in a completely different place now," she explains. "I've decided to more demonstratively articulate the issues within my marriage that bothered me."

While many of us report changes in interests, in jobs, and in career paths, others follow Rikki's lead and find ourselves reevaluating our lives in ways that may be subtler, but no less real. Other personal interactions may change for us as we move beyond the gravitational pull of our fathers. Sometimes these changes catch us unaware, and they can turn our worlds upside down if we are unprepared. Our relationships with our mothers, for example, may have seemed solid and independent. But few of us have factored in the influence of our fathers on this seemingly private bond, the weight of the third corner in the parental triangle. Even those of us who anticipated some change in our relationships with our surviving parents often report with surprise how the connection with our widowed mothers varies, particularly after the first crush of mourning has passed. Those of us whose parents separated or divorced often find this relationship changing as well. Especially if our fathers had remarried, we may find ourselves reevaluating the layers of connection and intimacy between ourselves and our stepparents, affiliations of affection but not of birth. Some of us will watch our widowed moms launched into singlehood with all the giddiness of sixteen-year-olds, a change that can be as heartbreaking for us as it seems to be invigorating for them. Others get to see women we had considered elderly and frail learn the confidence and joy of new independence.

"What's surprised me most is how my relationship with—and my view of—my *mother* has changed," says Jill, whose father died four years ago. "To see the way my mom has flowered—she's now seventy-five—has been amazing."

For still other women, the loss of our fathers has meant great shifts in our roles within the family. We may take on new responsibilities, *their* responsibilities, toward family members. For example, we may find ourselves becoming the caregivers for disabled or incapacitated siblings or for elderly mothers. We may also don, with these responsibilities, the strengths and capabilities that we had previously attributed only to men, or particularly to our fathers.

"My dad had always been the head of the household, and suddenly I was the 'man' of the family," says Ellen, whose father died three years ago. An only child, Ellen had been used to getting her own way. Athletic and assertive, she'd always been independent and free-spirited, several times leaving secure jobs on a whim for new cities and new adventures. And yet she automatically assumed the role her father left her before she realized that she had a choice. "I became very protective of my mother and I realized that, yes, I had to learn to do this stuff I had depended on my dad to do. Suddenly, I had to become a businessperson."

Sometimes we experience these new strengths in an opposite manner, letting ourselves shed familial expectations and burdens as we try on roles and lifestyles we'd never previously dared dream about. Often our awareness of the passage of time, of mortality, makes such experimentation a priority. "A year after he died I began writing creatively and attempting to be published," says one woman who introduced herself simply as "a homemaker" when we first began to talk. Her father had been a journalist, and during his life his accomplishments discouraged her from entering the field as a novice. "Right after he died, I aggressively sought out a more creative job," adds another, whose father had often denigrated her work in design.

For Felicity, who has held a steady job since graduating from college nearly twenty years ago, the death of her father four years ago has allowed her reevaluate her ready acceptance of her family's concern with stability. "Since my father died I have felt more urgent about freedom, about taking risks," she says. Childless by choice, she has few responsibilities to tie her to the stringent work ethic that she inherited from her large working-class family. "I've never wanted a nine-to-five job," she says now, and, for the first time in her life, she has felt free to research options. In the years since her father's death, she has been taking classes in stand-up comedy and jewelry making, and is now searching for a part-time position that will allow her to follow her heart.

None of this knowledge comes without a price. With the loss of our fathers we are bereft and often rudderless, at least for a while. Before we move on, we must mourn and come to terms with our loss. At times, perhaps for more of us than care to admit it, that includes accepting the end of the possibility of reconciliation. "My sister and I both privately believed that eventually there would come a time when we came to an understanding with Dad," recalls Rikki, thinking back to the long talks the two siblings had in the hospital lounge during their father's final illness. "That afternoon, when we realized it wasn't going to happen in that way, we were able to let go of that."

Without our fathers we also experience for the first, and perhaps the only, time in our lives a rare moment of feeling unencumbered—at liberty to choose our futures. Whether this will spur us on to have children, to finalize an emotional commitment, or break an outgrown bond, we cannot foretell. What we do know is that for the strongest of us, those of us willing to learn, this loss may be the first time we can clearly perceive our fathers' influences on us. And once we can decipher this influence, how we grew up interacting with them, and what we have lost with their deaths, this sad lesson can teach us the value of our own time. Our losses can help us recalibrate the settings of our own lives according to our adult needs and desires. We have always been our fathers' daughters. What comes next is learning how to merge this role with that of the women we may become.

CHAPTER 2

Reconciling Visions

December 1992

On my third visit to the hospital, my father offered me his rice pudding. The creamy dessert had not been removed when the orderly took his lunch tray. My father at first was afraid it had been, and wanted to call the young man back, but I found the pudding, still in its plastic container, on the counter by the sink. At his insistence, I had a spoonful. It tasted sweet, with a vague vanilla-cinnamon bite, and I thanked him for thinking of me.

For the past two days, I had been sitting with my father sometime close to his lunch hour. He had been hospitalized three days earlier in the final stages of cancer. This visiting time not only fit into my work schedule, but also allowed me to catch him at his still most lucid, before the morphine befuddled his otherwise sharp mind. I had been present when lunch was served the day before, and had commented (at a loss for other words) that the food looked quite decent, good for hospital food. He had agreed, insisting then, too, on giving me a taste of the custard that had followed his roast chicken.

Having food in his stomach seemed to clear his head, and after I put the rice pudding dish down we had a pretty good discussion. He asked about events in the outside world, about the fighting then going on in Somalia and the presidential transition. He talked about the discomfort of role reversal occasioned by his becoming a patient after forty-seven years as a doctor, and spoke sadly of the strange nightmares that stayed with him, disorienting him when he first awoke. Whether they sprang from his medications or the advancing stage of his illness, he didn't know. Sometimes, he admitted, embarrassed, he was no longer sure what had really happened and what he had dreamed. He asked if I had had my dessert.

Every American family, maybe every family, is fixated on eating to some extent. Ours, somewhere along the traditional Jewish spectrum of nurturing through food, certainly was. All through the years I'd lived at home, dinner centered the family. Unlike at some of my friends' houses, at our table nobody watched television during the evening meal; nobody read the paper then. Absence from dinner was acceptable only by permission, for a special event. Friends being invited to join us was a big deal.

Dinner was my mother's territory; my father was lord of treats. Almost until he was hospitalized, up to the last month when the cancer had infiltrated his bones and movement became painful, he would take charge of snacks when I dropped by. A little prerandial something, he would say, in case we're feeling peckish. Then he'd emerge from the galley kitchen of my folks' condo bearing a tray of garlic-bread rounds or melted Gruyère on toast. Sometimes, when I was little, he'd buy jelly doughnuts on his way back from Saturday morning hospital rounds. Most Sundays while I was growing up, he would pick up the Chinese food or the pizza we had ordered to give my mother a break. It was part of the treat that I'd get to go with him and hold the bag or the warm, flat box on the drive back.

For a few months before he was hospitalized, my father tended to reminisce in conversation. Had he told me, he would ask, about courting my mother with no money and only ten weeks before his Army call-up? Had he told me about arriving in Boston for college, fresh from Brooklyn and utterly confused by a local's direction to "take the Park Street under," the subway, to Harvard Square? He seemed eager to share this history, to share what he remembered of his parents and his grandparents, of growing up in Brooklyn in the same house as his aunts and uncles and stern grandmother. Sensing the comfort these stories brought, I encouraged him. And fighting my own reluctant acknowledgment of his condition, I brought along a tape recorder one afternoon to capture these memories before they were lost.

Wanting to connect this history with what I could recall, wanting to contribute to what seemed reassuring, I asked him once if he remembered our snow-walks. Our snow-walks had been a winter tradition, perhaps the treat I savored most because they couldn't be planned. They were totally weather-dependent. Whenever there had been a great snowfall, we would get ready. My father would have the family don coats and boots, urging us all into our winter wear with his great enthusiastic gestures, and we would all head out for an hour or so. Sometimes, if it was daylight, we would hike through the woods behind our house, along the stream that stayed black and unfrozen through much of the winter. If the snow had not let up until nightfall, or if he had been working, our walk would take place after dinner as he led us up the still, calm streets of our neighborhood.

These I liked best. I remember hiking up Luddington Road, which began a block past the house, and hearing him greet and be greeted by neighbors out shoveling paths and driveways in the light reflected off the snow. Such storms always made people seem friendlier. But these greetings were secondary to the real purpose of our walk. About a mile and a half, at most, when we'd turned off Luddington to Merrick and I was getting pretty tired, we would arrive at Richie's Deli. There we would have either toffees or apricot shoe leather peeled from a plastic roll. That was the treat.

Sitting in the hospital room, where my mother had joined us, I asked my father again about the snow-walks. He seemed to recall them, but not too clearly. He was thinking of other things, he said. He wanted to know if I thought the room was cold. Rather than ask for another blanket, my mother and I helped him into the purple plush sweatshirt I had brought as a Chanukah gift. He could hold himself in a sitting position for a moment, but it took both hands. While he held on to the bed rails, my mother and I worked the soft pullover down his body, rolling the hood into a pad behind his head.

"There," my mother said. "That's so much handsomer than the hospital johnny. You look like a football player who's injured his knee in the big game."

"Some knee," my father said. "Some game."

Neither of us had much to say to that, and my father's attention began to wander. He looked out the window, then closed his eyes. Perhaps lunch and our visit had tired him out; maybe the medications were kicking in. I needed to get to work. Before he could drift into sleep, I bent over the side of his bed. I told him I loved him and then kissed him. I told him I had enjoyed my treat. Half-asleep, he reached up and patted my cheek.

"Sweet," he said.

Valuing Ourselves

My father told me I was sweet but, as I've learned in the years since his death, it was perhaps more important that he thought I was intelligent. For our fathers' judgments of us—I have heard again and again from theorists, psychologists, and dozens of women—are what give us our first sense of ourselves. And in that mirror function, seeing ourselves in their eyes, I was in some ways very lucky. In many ways, my father was proud of me. Every accomplishment I could claim, every story I published, from my school newspaper up to the big-city dailies, was passed along to his colleagues and friends as if it were the Nobel Prize. "Your father's very proud of you," I remember one of his patients, a woman I had never before met, telling me when we were introduced one day in his office waiting room. "He showed me one of your articles."

Even when he was dying he couldn't resist bragging about me. Two weeks before his death in January 1993, as I walked through the hospital corridor to his room I recognized the type and design of my newspaper on the bulletin board by the nurses' station. Pinned to the board was a clipping from that day's paper, the essay that began this chapter: an essay I had written two nights before, after spending a tense lunch hour by his bedside and a thoughtful, sorrowful day at the office. I had written it for myself, I had told my editor, and I wasn't sure that it was appropriate for the paper. I could also have revealed that it was composed more as an excuse to stay late at the office and to avoid returning my mother's anxious phone calls than for any other reason. But I didn't, and I guess the words spoke for themselves: my editor had liked it. He had run it as one of an occasional series of first-person pieces that graced our features section, and I had been grateful for the outpouring of sympathy and support it had elicited from my colleagues, many of whom had already faced such family crises.

I had never thought about my father reading it. After all, the essay had portrayed him—*I* had portrayed him—in such a diminished light, as sick and weak and, worst of all for a man who prided himself on sensitivity and reason, as increasingly crabby in the face of his losing battle with cancer. I had never wanted him to see himself reflected in my eyes that way, and frankly I had thought he was too far gone, too woozy from his morphine, to still be reading the paper. When I saw it on the wall, I wasn't sure what to expect.

I needn't have worried. He was thrilled. "Did you see the article my daughter wrote?" He was lying in bed, too weak to sit up without assistance, but he was grilling the attendant who was readying him for lunch when I walked in. His doctor followed and I hung by the door, uneasy. "Did you get a copy?" my father asked the doctor as the younger man checked his charts. "I gave my copy to the nurses to post. And there she is now!" He'd spotted me, and so I came in to hug him, blushing from discomfort at the various layers of interaction going on around me. I was in this hospital as the child of a patient, having publicized his weakness in my professional capacity. I saw the doctor's eyes, his still, set face silently acknowledging the truth of the despair and decline I had written about, while right beside us my father chortled with glee. My father, this dying man, was bragging about his daughter—me. I felt uncomfortable, exposed. But I also felt warm inside with a glow that nothing else at that time could give me. I knew that once again, and perhaps for the last time, I had made my father proud.

Self-image, many experts say, is one of the primary gifts that daughters receive from their fathers, and self-esteem—or the lack of it—may perhaps be the major legacy left to us after we lose our fathers. We can learn love from our mothers, the theory runs. But we must learn to value ourselves from our fathers. The reason is distance; our mothers, closer to us and more nurturing since before our birth, are not in a position to judge us—our fathers are. As they see us, so we learn to see ourselves, with all the components of value and worth that such an outside evaluation implies. Freud had theorized this link in terms of sexuality and "feminization." In our version of the Oedipal complex, he wrote, little girls learn to be feminine, like their mothers, in order to attract the love of their fathers. This process, theoretically, frees us from the potentially smothering mother-daughter bond and—as we learn to displace our attraction from our fathers to other men—teaches how to function as adults, which, in this conservative theory, specifically means heterosexual adults. Although the generations since Freud tend to reject as outdated and sexist the idea that we grow into our sense of "femininity" by trying to please, if not seduce, our fathers, the basic idea that our fathers are our first mirrors still makes sense. Being the first others in our lives, our fathers act as our proving grounds, helping us develop our "sense of personal effectiveness," as Henry Biller writes in *Fathers and Families*. Simply by being the other-gendered parent, they fulfill this role, whatever our ultimate sexual orientation turns out to be.

Even as our society changes, as fathers take on more of the nurturing childcare roles and mothers more quickly resume their jobs and duties in the outside world, this paradigm holds. Not only do our mothers carry us for nine months and bear us, forging a link that cannot be denied, but for most of our generation (women who are now adults and who have come to adulthood beginning with the feminist movement of the 1970s) our mothers were still usually the primary caretakers of our childhood. And they are women, like us. No matter how different our lives may be, in many ways we patterned ourselves on—or forged our identities as reactions against—who they were as wives and mothers, who they were as women. We saw, and even years after their death, continue to see, ourselves in them.

Our fathers, however, were the first outsiders and, even if they were the ones who raised us, the first distinctly different people in our lives. They were usually—and on this Freud seems to have voiced a lasting truth—our first great opposite-gender loves. From them, from their care and concern and time with us, we still gauge our setpoints for how much we are worth, or how little. Our mothers were our allies, but our fathers were the ones who helped set our self-esteem. "Since he is the 'other,'" writes Linda Schierse Leonard in *The Wounded Woman*, "he . . . shapes her differentness, her uniqueness and individuality."

This is a distinctly different role from the one our mothers play in our lives, and that difference grows to define the relationship. "Often there's more of a companionate relationship from daughter to mother. There's also the identification and the need to differentiate. That's less strong between daughters and fathers," says Froma Walsh, a professor at the University of Chicago and an editor of *Living Beyond Loss*.

When we talk of our fathers, we talk about our value. Goals and achievements—the manifestation of our worth—almost always come into play. "He's the one I wanted to make proud," one woman tells me, echoing dozens of others who have focused on their accomplishments when discussing their fathers. "My mother would love everything I did, but he was the one who questioned and who I wanted to please."

Even if we have internalized this code, we expect judgment. When it is missing, we note its absence as we wouldn't necessarily do in connection with our mothers. "He was always supportive in whatever way he could be," says Rachel, who since her father's death ten years ago has followed in his footsteps, completing her doctorate and becoming an academic just as he was. "Even before I went back to school, he was never critical. It was just not an issue." She acts as if this is a surprise.

Rachel is one of the lucky ones. Far from being uncritical, her father was instead unboundedly optimistic. He cared about what she did, but he believed that she would choose well. Although many factors play into her success, particularly her financial and intellectual ability to return to school, Rachel, now thirty-nine, believes that because of her father's confidence in her she, too, saw all things as possible. "I think, underneath it all, of what enormous pleasure this gave him," she says of her gradual shift from high school dropout to night school to full-time classes and finally to the prestigious Wellesley College. "I was doing what I was supposed to be doing: fulfilling my potential."

Because of his support, she says, "I have internalized an incredibly strong set of standards and directions from him," she says now, on the eve of defending her dissertation. "I believe if you start something you should finish it."

After her father's death, Ellen, too, found out just how much her father had believed in her. He was a difficult, argumentative man, but she always sensed that he was the source of her considerable strength as a sportswoman (a bicycle racer) as well as a successful player in the highly competitive world of magazine journalism. Sure enough, after his funeral, when she was cleaning out the cluttered office he had kept in their family home, she was pleasantly surprised to find file folders full of her work, from grade school papers up through records of each of her professional accomplishments. "He had saved all my report cards and everything I'd ever written," recalls Ellen. She found he had made multiple copies of one story, the first that had been published in one big-name publication. "He'd sent around about twenty copies," she notes now. "He was so proud of me."

I remember how, when we were talking, Ellen became quiet at this point. Whether lost in memories or fighting back tears I couldn't tell, but we were able to sit with this silence a little bit. We both understood what she had just said.

Paradoxical Roles

Of course, the women of our era—adults from our twenties into our fifties—also had a more timely reason to look for ourselves in our father's reflection. As these stories imply, the connections we maintained with our fathers once we left home were often based on work or education. We may have discussed love and romance with our mothers, but schools and jobs were areas that our fathers, usually much more than our mothers, had made their own. And now they are ours as well.

We are a hinge generation: women brought up largely by stay-at-home moms who tend to work outside the homes as our fathers did. As a result, we often looked to our dads more than our mothers as we learned how to navigate day-to-day lives in a world shaped by feminism and the modern economy. Although physically and perhaps emotionally we were more like our mothers, they could not, as a rule, be the professional role models we needed. And so, although we were female, we had to turn toward our fathers to provide that understanding. Our fathers were the ones who could relate to the particulars of job stress and boredom,

the meetings and deadlines and production quotas that we met—
that often we were the first women in our families to meet. In this
way, the women of our generation acted like sons, more treasured
and peculiar sons, because while we went into the workplace—
their world—we were still their daughters, their darlings.

But for many women of our generation, this fatherly pride, this
perfect seeing of us, ultimately led to conflict as we entered their
worlds. We are caught in what psychoanalyst Jessica Benjamin
calls a cultural divide, a split between past and present. We are
jumping from the traditional female roles, in which we tend
toward being accommodating, and the new modes of being effi-
cient, independent, and good at our jobs, which we learned by
watching our fathers. Our fathers defined us because they were
different from us, and in breaking with the traditional duties of
daughters we sought to emulate them as well as to please them.
This new growth had to evoke complicated, even contradictory,
responses. And true enough, our fathers' pride in us often ran
counter to their paternal desire to protect us, to rule over us as
patriarchs have traditionally ruled over daughters. The two roles
of a father—to be proud and to protect—have collided in discord
that stayed with many of us, at least throughout our fathers' lives.
This has left, for many of us, a patrimony of confusion and
betrayal that we may only begin to sort out after they have gone.

I remember running head-on into that conflict, and I remember how much it hurt. The confrontation happened when I was in
my mid-twenties, several years before my father's death. At that
time I was at a career crossroads. I had a steady job working in the
development office of a suburban college, a desk-bound position
that bored me so much I thought my eyes would cross each time I
had to start a new project. Since college, I had worked at the
wordsmithing of journalism and publishing, and had advanced my
career in a way that is common for my field. As often as I waited
for promotion at some publication, I also maneuvered my way into
more responsibility and increasingly interesting duties by changing jobs, trading in a freelance position at a city daily for a staff job

as a magazine arts editor, for example, and when I had become that small monthly's editor and served a year, jumping to a weekly newspaper as an associate editor.

My father had applauded each move as a triumph, a step toward the success he seemed to believe lay waiting for me. But I had run into a snag at my latest newspaper post: my boss had been fired, and the new boss and I didn't see eye to eye. Had I been laboring at the weekly newspaper for a decade, perhaps I would have built up some loyalty and the situation would have been salvageable. But with just one year at my current position there, I was asked to resign. I had been grateful to jump to the college job then, exhausted by weeks of verbal fencing during the transition. I even thought that leaving this kind of newspaper journalism might be a good move, giving me a break from deadlines and the stress of pleasing advertisers as well as editors with each new issue. I had not realized how much I had loved the energy of that life, the vibrant immediacy that was the upside of all the stress. I had not foreseen how soon a "relaxing" job would become unchallenging, how quickly my quiet suburban office and nine-to-five routine would grow stifling after the hustle and bustle of a city paper. I began looking for a way out.

"I'm thinking of getting back to newspapers," I said as I lay on my bed, ready for a leisurely phone conversation with my parents one Sunday night, my usual night to check in with them. "I'm considering going freelance again." I had supported myself as a freelance writer, along with a variety of part-time clerical jobs, for my first few years after college. My income during that period fluctuated, but I always managed to pay my rent and my bills. I was proudly aware of the fact that once I started working, I had never asked my parents for financial help and that for the past few years I had been living quite comfortably in my own two-bedroom apartment in a neighborhood that I liked. "I think I could do well freelance."

"Aren't you doing that already?" I could hear the anxiety in my father's voice. He was right; I had begun selling stories and critical essays again, which he knew because he collected all my clippings. But because I was also working full-time at the college, I was only able to write occasionally. Although my job did not require much in terms of brain power, it did take up my days, and for the longer pieces I wanted to investigate and write, nights and weekends weren't sufficient. Even if I could do without sleep, few official sources would be available after the normal business day, and most libraries have limited evening hours. I began to explain these limitations to him.

"Jobwise I'm fine. But there's no real future here. And I can't write with this job, not real pieces, the big ones. I figure if I can pull in a major magazine piece a month, I'll be fine, and I'd be back in line for a magazine job again." I sat up, aware of the tension growing as my voice began to tighten. To me, my plan seemed sensible: a calculated risk as I jumped back into an arena that I knew reasonably well. But, sensible young woman that I was, I was looking to downplay the risk in any way possible. And my parents had always voiced support of my career moves.

"I've got a favor to ask, though." When I had called my parents, I had been toying with the idea of asking them for help. I had not thought this would be a big deal, just a safety blanket. But now warning bells were going off in my head. Perhaps specifically because I wanted their reassurance, the confidence in me that I heard being questioned, I jumped in. "I think I'm okay financially, I mean, I can get as many small pieces as I can handle and I'm assuming I can get some decent assignments within three months. But, I just want to make sure I'm covered in case of an emergency. I've got one month in expenses put by, but I figure it could take about eight weeks to find another job like this one, if I really had to. So, if I had to, could I borrow $600 from you?" This would be another month's expenses, as I figured, the most I would ever need. Small change to my father, a prosperous physician in private practice.

"Absolutely not." His response was immediate. "You will not give up a steady job that gives you security and health insurance just so you can gallivant around." I had worked outside the home since I was sixteen, had supported myself since graduating from college. Several of my friends from similar middle-class backgrounds were returning to graduate school then, with help from their parents.

"I'm not asking you to pay for grad school." I tried that approach.

"I will not hear of it." He sounded angry now. "Don't behave like a child. I will not discuss this any further. Good night." He hung up the phone. I think I may have made some small talk with my mother, but basically the call was over. And as I sat there on my own bed, in my own apartment, surrounded by furnishings and possessions I had paid for, I suddenly felt like a child, a naughty little girl caught masquerading in a grownup's clothes. I was incapable of movement for much of the evening, and the emotional inertia stayed with me. I felt unable to leave that job for another six months, at which point I stumbled into a position at a newspaper that let me edit, but not write.

Even now, a decade later, I feel embarrassed revealing how much this exchange hurt me, as though it reveals the depth to which my parents, my father in particular, spoiled me. How many young women, for example, can consider leaving a steady full-time job? How many parents could afford to loan or give hundreds of dollars to their children? I assumed so much; I was asking for too much. I was acting like a child, like a spoiled little girl. Of course, my father was right.

But when I examine my hurt and my shock after that phone call, I see the other truths in that conversation. I was not being foolish; I did have a plan. I was not going untried into a new field or chasing an untested dream. I was looking for parental support to reenter an insecure but customary mode of employment for writers. I had no children, no mortgage, no responsibility beyond myself, which meant I was in the best possible position to assume such a risk. I was willing to gamble with security in order to try for a better future. I was willing to fail, to go back to part-time secretarial work if I had to. That was not the issue. What I was asking for was a pledge of security in case of an emergency, a financial vote of confidence as I contemplated how I could begin to climb back toward my dream. And my father, who had the money, and who had always and often expressed his belief in my abilities as a writer, was not willing to give me that. He did not suggest a compromise—helping me if I went into a graduate writing program, perhaps—or ask for more details of how I planned to enact my comeback as a writer. He was not interested in hearing about the feasibility of my plan, or in suggesting a less risky step that would be acceptable to both of us. Within a few minutes he had stepped out of the role of supportive, proud father into that of the stern patriarch, the one who knew what was best for me, and how that should be enacted with no interruption or input from me. And I had opened myself up to this treatment by asking for his help, being the child to his stern Daddy. No wonder, then, that I was used to this dichotomy. No wonder I fell into line.

Years later, when I recalled this conversation to my mother, she seemed not to remember it. "He said that?" she asked me when I was done, more for confirmation than out of surprise. Yes, he did, I told her. And during a subsequent phone conversation he had again switched into his patriarch mode, refusing to listen to any modifications of my plan. "He could be like that," she recalled then, sadly. "He worried a lot, you know."

And then she said the words that shocked me and, perhaps retroactively, made all my reactions clear. "I would have helped you," she continued. "I would have seen it as investment."

My mother was addressing me as an adult, as a woman like herself. And that helped me to understand what my father had not done, perhaps could not, do. Instead, my father had fallen into the second role that fathers often take. He was unwilling or incapable of seeing me as an adult, and, instead of assuming his usual role of doting daddy, he was playing the part of the unbending patriarch. At best, in this role the father is a protector, a brave defender ready to fight for his child (no matter how inappropriate his actions are to the age or independence of the players). At its less generous extreme, the patriarch is a tyrant who exercises control through gender roles, financial clout, and sometimes sheer physical size over the women and children of his family, and most particularly over a female child.

This cruel pairing of support and abandonment seems unnatural. However, it is only one of the many paradoxes in their relationship that fathers and daughters face and, if they are lucky, grow through together. The roles are linked, opposite sides of the same behavior. Think about the stereotype of "Daddy's little girl." In that scenario a cherished little girl is spoiled by a doting dad who believes the world is barely good enough for her. In some lights, that father will fulfill his first role admirably; he will have such pride in his darling that he will instill in her the self-confidence to fulfill her potential despite any obstacle. She will become the strong daughter of a proud father. But in that same scenario she is also the precious baby who needs to be protected (because she is a child, if not because she is a girl) against the outside world and, perhaps, herself.

Follow this scenario through and we see how easily the adoring father can become the overprotective parent or the stern patriarch. Both sets of roles have such attraction for both the father and the daughter, weighted in family and social tradition as well as in the natural desires to protect and defend, to be coddled and taken care of. At first, when the daughter is a child, the parental urge to call all the shots is natural and healthy. For the daughter, the desire to be cared for and found special is compelling and seductive—and may continue to be, even when adult independence makes such a degree of care unnecessary. How does this relationship coexist with the proud-parent–happy-daughter partnership designed to foster self-esteem? For many of us, the two bump unhappily side by side, and are never totally resolved even when we have grown beyond any need for our fathers' aid or guidance. And this split, the "good daddy/rigid patriarch," is only one possibility of how these dual roles can manifest themselves. Many women tell of fathers who expressed the conflicting desire to launch their daughters and also to protect or control them.

"He was very critical by nature, as most journalists are," recalls Stella, who despite her father's harsh dismissal of her work, followed him into the newspaper business. Despite his unkind critiques, she recalls—ten years after his death—that once she began to build her career, "he took obvious delight in my success. Especially when we were both working at the same big-city newspaper and his colleagues would compliment my writing to him.

"At one point I went out on strike with the newspaper's union and he crossed the picket line. Everyone at the paper assumed this would cause a rift between us, but in fact it's an episode I remember fondly because our relationship was so strong at that point and so full of mutual respect that we didn't even have any friction over our separate decisions. We would joke about it," she now recalls.

For other women, these two roles collided in less positive, less affectionate ways.

" 'Stupid' was his favorite word," says Irina, talking about her father. Her stormy relationship with her dad was rarely without shouting before his death seven years ago. "Why do you want to go into consulting, you're so stupid?" she remembers him asking her rhetorically. "Why did you buy that stupid car?"

Despite such emotional abuse, Irina—a tall, elegant woman in her late forties—has emerged as a strong professional who has recently left a managerial job to establish her own firm. After a decade of therapy, she says, she has learned to work through the misguided and hurtful criticism from her father. In some ways, she says, she learned strength from such attacks. These days she looks back at how she fought with him, the way she mastered the ability to match him, verbal blow for verbal blow. She sees in these exchanges the beginning of the perseverance that would make her a success in business, albeit at a great emotional cost. The reason she has managed to come through such abuse, she now believes, and what helped keep her courage up during the years of such interchanges, was hearing how he talked of her to others. "To my face, he would call me stupid," she can remember, almost fondly. "But on the phone to his friends I would always hear him bragging about me!"

At its emotional core, the conflict is ancient. Although our current financial and professional stature has brought it into high relief, the basic face-off may be seen in classic works of art from centuries past. Call it the Brunnhilde factor, for in Wagner's great nineteenth-century opera cycle, the conflict between the god Wotan and his favorite daughter, the Valkyrie Brunnhilde, is one that many of us would recognize today. In brief, Wotan is the classic doting daddy; he has always praised Brunnhilde's accomplishments, her warlike (and thus dadlike) approach, and encouraged her to be, well, almost like him. He has such confidence in Brunnhilde that, in *Die Valkyrie*, he entrusts her with the task of protecting the hero Siegmund (who is also her half-brother, but that's a different story). But after he gives her specific instructions to guard the hero, Wotan is prevailed upon by others to let Siegmund die. He then calls his daughter back and gives her a new command, ordering her to let the hero be killed. This is where the conflict begins: Brunnhilde has been witness to her father's original reasoning. Plus, she has been encouraged to be strong and somewhat independent, and she knows her father well enough to recognize that he truly loves Siegmund. In short, she uses her own judgment. She intervenes to save the mortal hero, and earns her father's wrath. "But I was just doing as you truly wished," she responds (in loose translation) when confronted with her disobedience. "I am your will." No matter. Although it clearly breaks both their hearts, Wotan takes away Brunnhilde's goddess status and banishes her forever from his presence. Because she has acted as a strong daughter, as the goddess and Valkyrie she is, she is both beloved by her father and ultimately rejected by him. That she is banished from her father's palace, made mortal, and "condemned" to love a mortal man perhaps illustrates the best resolution of such a situation, when the father assumes godlike proportions and the daughter has grown up strong. Perhaps for all of us with autocratic fathers, this permanent farewell is necessary before we can leave the narcissistic family circle and become real adult—that is, mortal—women.

Conflicts

This paradox is at the center of the father-daughter relationship. In a way, this conflict—dependence versus freedom—springs from the same roots as our self-esteem issues, from the earliest tensions between ourselves and the outside world, as represented by our fathers. As I've already noted, our fathers are separate from us, but they also serve to reflect us. They must encourage us, but they also must protect us. For us from our earliest days, they represent the outside world, both as models for what we can do and become and as its gatekeepers, its mediators, the ones who let us go or told us when to stop.

The roots of what may prove to be a lifelong conflict lie in early childhood, say theorists and psychologists. And our fathers may hold the key in the battle between our earliest desire for independence and our yearning to be recognized and loved. It is important to recall at this point that traditionally, in all our cultural myths, our mothers are the constant, nurturing influence, whereas our fathers get to be the "other," the free parents, the ones who can leave. It is this freedom—a liberty usually embodied by our fathers—that young children yearn for as they begin to explore and develop independent identities, psychoanalyst Jessica Benjamin writes in *Like Subjects, Love Objects*.

We realize this early on: our fathers are not as connected as we are. They are not tied to the home the way our mothers are. They are able to leave and then to come back into the warmth and security of the house without being penalized, and we envy their secure and confident mobility. They are, as Benjamin and others explain, the "coming and going" parents. They are free, as our mothers and we as young children are not, to realize their own desires.

This freedom is not linked purely to the ideal of nuclear family. Although many of us were raised in the traditional nuclear grouping, with only our fathers working outside of the house, this role is more basic than some familial stereotype. The quality of "agency," that is the ability to move in the world, is not inherently connected with masculinity or traditional family roles. Instead, it is linked more closely with the primal physical bond a child has with its mother. For nine months, the mother is there, the first physical presence that a baby knows. Often still, even in families where the mother has an active career, the first few months of our lives are in the care of our mothers. And in our society, these roles are backed by socially approved duties: our mothers exist to accommodate, please, and feed us. Our fathers primarily act independently. Although some of our societal patterns are changing, a father still tends to be the one who can safely leave, and just as safely return.

As we grow, as we see our capabilities in his eyes and begin to feel our own strength, we want to emulate him. We want to go, as long as we, too, have the security of knowing we can return. We think, "I love him because I want to be like him—free to come and go." But we are not like our fathers. We are children, we are female. And therein lies the struggle.

Some of this conflict arises partly as a process of development, since this natural growth is pit against our very real childhood need to be protected, even as we explore our independence. But this conflict is exacerbated, say family theorists, because of the significant inability of fathers to allow their daughters to explore, experiment, and venture into the world. The problem may not even necessarily be what fathers forbid daughters, but rather what they simply forget to teach us. Several theorists (including Michael Lamb and Jessica Benjamin) have noted that fathers are more likely to form an intense bond of identification with sons than with daughters. As role models, they are much more likely to encourage independent growth, particularly agency, in their sons than in their daughters, to our great loss.

Growing girls and young women therefore must untangle a string of confused goals and mixed messages. We look to our fathers to help us figure out who to be, and we try to work out what we want for ourselves. Often there is no way to meet all these expectations, and we end up feeling as if we are the ones who have failed.

"He really wanted to baby me," says Jill, whose father passed away four years ago. "When I left for school, he became really solicitous, wanting to give me all this stuff—candy, money, whatever."

Although her parents' marriage was stormy, Jill says it was his overprotectiveness, not her parents' screaming fights, that made her want to flee. "I remember him yelling at my mother and throwing a coffee cup. I think back on that and that seems very real. I find that kind of anger very easy to understand. The other thing—always giving us money—that made me sort of cringe. It made me feel sort of suffocated, and I couldn't accept it. I think that's a huge reason we grew apart," she now says.

"He wanted me to be independent, but not too independent," adds Rikki. "He always told me I was his biggest fan, which was flattering as a young girl but became burdensome as I matured."

This complex relationship became thornier when Rikki, now in her late thirties, dropped out of college to marry and have a family. "I believe he would have wanted me to finish college and have a more stimulating and rewarding career," she now says. "I always felt he was disappointed in me somehow."

"Encourage me? Well, he came to my college graduation. But I don't really think he did very much verbally," Valerie says. Forty-eight and never married, Valerie feels her life has been somewhat empty, more disconnected from people and children and love than she would have liked. She takes all the responsibility onto herself, however, and when she first looks back on the father who passed away twenty years ago she describes him as a gentle and kind-hearted man.

But as she examines her life closely, looking for the details that could support her initial impression, that picture changes. She begins to see how unable or unwilling he was to become engaged in her life as an adult. Unlike Irina, who suffered verbal abuse but was also able to take some comfort in her father's grudging pride, Valerie felt emotionally abandoned—unable to get any kind of response from her cool, detached father. She tends to accept his coolness as a judgment on her failures: she did not fulfill his view of what a woman should do, that is, get married and raise a family. "He was very proud of my other sisters, at their weddings, all four of them before me," she recalls with a touch of regret. "I was the first one who didn't get married." Juxtaposing this memory with the perceived inadequacies of her own life she wonders, perhaps for the first time, how his narrow expectations played into both the love she "failed" to find, and her own preoccupation with her single status.

Jacqui, who did fulfill her father's traditional goals by marrying and raising two children before his death last year, now wonders how much his limited dreams for her constrained her own hopes for herself. Although she knows herself to be a bright and well-organized woman, Jacqui has been having trouble refocusing her energies now that her children are nearly grown. She finds herself longing for more direction in life, for some projects for the next stage. And she wonders how much she inherited her father's limitations along with his love. "I think my dad's failings for me were that he did not have real ambitions for me. The priority was on my brothers. My big brother was the star of the family. The eggs were in his basket."

Jacqui admits to feeling rather lost since her father's death, and spends much of her time contemplating not only what she will do next but also how to motivate herself. How much of her aimlessness stems from her father's stunted and perhaps confused ambitions for her, she may never really know. "I think I had a lot more to offer than he realized," she recognizes now. Although he is gone, she continues to work on the legacy of her bond with her father and his vision of her.

For me, eight years after the death of my father, what remains is both the love and the shock of betrayal as time and time again he brought me up short. I can clearly recall his great faith in me, the confidence of a gentle man who brought me treats and who told me on his deathbed that I was sweet. And just as I lose myself in memories like these, I find myself interrupted by the other image, also true, that I tended to suppress during his life: the stern father whose word was law, who saw me as an unruly child in need of guidance, if not discipline. Even now, eight years later, I still have trouble reconciling these images. I am still haunted by what they mean about who I am, woman and daughter and wife.

The truth is that the father-daughter relationship does not disappear, nor is it resolved when women lose their fathers. Perhaps all that disappears with this loss is the ability to alter this relationship, to change the image of ourselves that we see reflected in our fathers' eyes. Which may be why, as we begin to evaluate the changes in our own lives, we must first step back and examine this relationship, how it was manifest as we were growing up, how it affected us, and what it has left to us. "The death of the father does not end the relationship," concludes Froma Walsh, echoing the thoughts we share in our memories and our tales. "That continues on in the mind of the survivor."

CHAPTER 3

Fatherless Girls

Statistics show that it is likely that we will lose our fathers years before we lose our mothers, and researchers discuss how important such a loss is throughout the life cycle. Although this book focuses primarily on women who have lost their fathers after reaching adulthood, this chapter examines the impact of losing a father during childhood or adolescence. By discussing these earlier losses, we will learn more about the father-daughter relationship throughout our life cycle and more deeply understand why our fathers come to represent so many different things to us.

The moments when I miss my father most are not the ones I expected. Yes, I do wish he could have been at my wedding. I would probably still have opted to walk by myself to the sheltering canopy of the chuppah where my fiance and friends waited, but it would have been good to have him there as well, by my mother's side. Yes, I wish he had been able to see the first home we purchased, although the two of us were so exhausted by packing and moving that our first week in the lovely old building was marred by the temper and clumsiness of fatigue. These milestones and the others that are to come would have been good times to share with him, and I can summon in my mind the image of the beaming smile he would have bestowed on me. I can imagine the pride he'd have had in me and in the happy turns my life has taken.

But the days and nights when I miss my father most are not these big-ticket events, which tend to buzz and flush with their own excitement and stand so far outside normal time as to defy any expected family context. I miss him more, I find, in the unexpected moments that remind me of how he was in day-to-day life. The discovery of a volume on maritime history at a used-book sale, for example, can make my throat close up momentarily as I recall how he'd settle in after dinner with just such a treasure. The appearance of soft-shell crabs in spring or a perfect plate of thumbnail-size cherrystone clams, glistening and fresh on a summer day, brings his hearty appetite to mind. The aging appearance of one of his favorite actors, with new wrinkles and a balding pate my father never got to see, makes me—just for the moment—sad.

These are the details that bring my father back to me, and also remind me of my loss. It's these facts of our life together, rather than the milestones that I have marked since his passing, that cause me to remember my father most and to miss him. I find it hard to imagine what my life would be like, or what my loss would feel like, if I did not have these tangible memories. I regret not having my father here to witness more about my life, to see how I turned out, but I know that I am lucky to have had the opportunity to know him, to have had his presence through much of my growing years.

Early Loss

Clearly, not all of us are so lucky. The early death of a parent is no longer as common as it may have been, but it still affects a large segment of the population. As researchers who study father-daughter relationships point out, many more young children "lose" their fathers to divorce or abandonment than to death, but for the 6 percent of single-mother households that are fatherless because of the father's death (using the numbers provided in David Popenoe's *Life Without Father*), the effect is overwhelming, and anecdotal evidence from women who have grown up fatherless resonates with this tragedy.

Sometimes the effect was practical: the aftershocks of such a loss may have thrown us into different worlds because of the upheaval of the family's finances or because of changing employment needs. Often it was more subtle: a father's premature death may have influenced our development in quiet ways, altering years later how we work and whom we love, basically intruding into all aspects of who we have turned out to be. This loss, in other words, may be as influential as our fathers would have been, with the added impact of early trauma. Depending on our age and on the circumstances that surrounded us at the time of our bereavement, we may still be dealing with our grief and the gaping wounds it made in our lives a half century later.

For many women who lost their fathers very young, the very idea of a father—of what fathering may mean—is intriguing. It occupies our thoughts like a sore tooth, which we worry without always meaning to. It is where we ache. "I often watch fathers with their children," says Donna, whose father died forty-five years ago, when she was three. "I think fathering means that you get a kind of male perspective that I didn't get; you get a male perspective on life that is really, really important. And you get a sense of toughness." She sits back to think about her own words, and then explains: "I watched one of my male friends coach his eleven-year-old daughter on how to negotiate for a higher salary for babysitting. She got on the phone and did it. She was terrified, but she did it, and I thought, 'That's what dads do. They really help you with those skills.' "

Not that Donna is entirely missing such practical skills. Despite her early loss, Donna has learned to negotiate the world. She is now a psychiatrist affiliated with a prestigious private hospital. She has a fancy title and earns a good salary, and she has clearly been able to compensate in a practical way for the lack of this early parenting. However, she has never stopped thinking about what she did not get. "There is this pride that a father has that I have never experienced," she says. For Donna, having a father would have meant having an ally, a teacher who could decipher how the practical world operates. To some extent, Donna says, this is a lack she has felt throughout her life.

"I think it's made me sort of limited," says Yael, commenting on the loss of her father, who died when she was six. "I'm limited because I'm sexist, in the way that men can be sexist about women. But I'm sexist about men, against men." Uncomfortable around men, with a visceral unease she believes dates from her father's death and the debilitating illness that began to remove him from her life years earlier, she describes how she has built a life that is almost entirely devoid of men and of male influences: "I read mostly novels written by women. I judge most movies in terms of how they relate to women. My whole way of being is kind of geared toward limiting myself in a certain sense." She acknowledges that this prejudice is not based on experience. If anything, she believes, it is based on lack of experience—on a lack of contact with men she could respect and relate to on any real emotional level. And because she holds a high position in a professional field that employs many men, she realizes that her prejudice may cause her to discriminate. She tries to be careful, to be aware of the effect of her discomfort. "It's something I have to work on," she says. "It's what I have to work on in this lifetime."

Yael and Donna are not alone. Studies on the emotional effects of a father's death on young children reveal just how debilitating this early loss can be to a woman's entire emotional outlook. To begin with, consider all that happens when we are children, all that we do and experience. Childhood is when we spend most of our time learning and experimenting, all of which happens at an amazing pace. There's a lot going on at every age, and it is sequential: we build our education on what we already know. We develop into a new stage only after completing the stage before.

Trauma of any sort, however, breaks into this normal growth, toppling the building blocks of safe experimentation that we assemble into our lives. A crisis like the death of one's father, for example, may disturb a young girl's progression through psychological stages where she learns attachment and love. Ultimately, with that lesson disrupted, this loss may injure the development of her individual and independent identity. Such disruption is not peculiar to the loss of a parent. Family traumas such as the death or serious illness of a sibling, for example, or an attack or an injury on the child herself may have a similar effect. In a way, a trauma derails a child. Speeding along through growth stages, a child who hits a crisis of this magnitude may get thrown off track during a particular stage of development. Once off track, it can be very difficult to resume progress. Often, in fact, such children find themselves stuck at particular developmental levels for years, if not permanently, unable to complete the psychological task that she had begun when the crisis occurred. The child may grow into a seemingly healthy adult, but with something left undone she may find herself vulnerable, unable to function in some deep emotional way, and that leaves her unsatisfied with who she is. The younger the child is—both common sense and research support—the greater the damage, but children of any age suffer terribly when either parent is taken from them.

Parents—by which I mean a stable adult presence, whether by birth, adoption, or some other arrangement—are a vital part of an undisturbed, nurturing childhood: a young girl develops her personality against the safe, steady backdrop of her parents and home. In the traditional family setup, she can cling to her mother and then her father as an infant and young child, learn to differentiate herself from them as an older child, and discover that she may safely leave them as an adolescent. The continued presence of her parents as stable points of reference allows her to navigate these stages safely. When one or both of her parents (or any adult from whom the child has learned love and trust) are removed, however, this safe journey becomes much rockier, and its progression much less sure.

In families that get split by divorce, the causes and costs are complicated. For example, children of divorce often seem to have more problems in school and with antisocial behavior. But it is not always clear if a child's disruptive and sometimes self-destructive behavior—violence or its opposite, social withdrawal, for example—would have occurred in an unhappy but intact marriage, in which the parents remained in the same house but fought constantly. The one finding that researchers tend to link to divorce specifically is that young girls whose fathers have left the family tend to "act out" with excessive and early sexual behavior toward men. Of course, even this finding does not make its cause clear. Such girls, and this behavior has been reported by several researchers, may be overreacting to their anxiety around men, overcompensating for their fear or discomfort. Or they may be acting on the misconception that the divorce was the result of their being rejected, and that a happier family may be obtained by "winning" a man back. Whatever the reasons, the price such fatherless girls pay is high.

In families where a parent dies, different kinds of breakdowns in the normal process of growth are common. The loss of a father due to death may make girls more dependent, according to some researchers. For example, Frances L. Turnbull's 1991 study of twenty-four adults who had lost a parent between the ages of seven and seventeen showed that girls who had lost fathers tended to regress into earlier, more childlike behaviors than would be customary among their peers.

This is markedly different from what researchers find with girls who lose their mothers. Although that loss is arguably more devastating, with possibly greater impact on a girl's healthy development, it does not tend to throw an older child—or young woman—back into childhood in the same way. Turnbull's observations found that father loss in particular interfered with young girls' move toward independence. Her study, which contained more daughters who had lost fathers than bereaved sons or daughters who had lost mothers, offers several suggestions for this regression. One factor may be the behavior of bereaved parents: Widowed fathers, for example, tend to seek support from outside the family, such as by finding a girlfriend. Widowed mothers, however, are more likely to turn inward, to lean on their children for support. According to Turnbull's study, such behavior may urge a growing and increasingly independent young girl into an earlier, more infantilized state, as a means of comforting both her mother and herself.

"The revival of dependency needs and regressive longings was more strongly associated with father loss than with mother loss," Turnbull writes.

Psychotherapist and author Michele Bograd, who lost her father when she was fourteen, points out that the mother's reaction, the way she "mediates" the death, so to speak, may also have deep repercussions. How the mother remembers the deceased— for example if she refuses to acknowledge his flaws—may make accepting and understanding the death more difficult. In addition, if she was able to provide information while the father was ill or dying, she may be able to help her child cope with the loss. In opposition to Turnbull's findings, Bograd believes that in some cases—as when a mother seems incapacitated by grief—the death of a father may rush a child into maturity as she assumes emotional responsibility for her bereaved mother. With either reaction, the normal growth and development is disturbed, and this data lends scientific weight to the longing that women such as Donna describe simply as "Daddy hunger."

For Donna, who lost her father during what most psychological theorists consider a crucial phase of attachment to her parents, this hunger has haunted her. Losing her father at the age of three meant Donna never finished the task of that age, which includes learning to love in a healthy, giving-and-receiving manner. In strict Freudian terms, which Donna favors, she never resolved the Oedipal conflict. She feels she never worked through the classic childhood desire to replace her same-gender parent (her mother) as the mate of the opposite-gender parent (her father). Her father was gone too soon. And because she never got to act this out in a healthy fashion, she believes she has continued to replay this drama in inappropriate and unsafe ways ever since.

When she was an older child, Donna believes, this unresolved longing made her particularly vulnerable. Looking for a father replacement through her preteen years, she found herself responding to any older man who gave her attention—making her an easy target, she now believes, for the pedophile who raped her when she was eleven years old.

Unfortunately, her experience supports what researchers such as David Popenoe believe. As Popenoe, a professor of sociology at Rutgers University, concludes in *Life Without Father*, girls in fatherless households are more likely to suffer abuse; they are much more likely to be the victims of rapists and child molesters. Some women believe, as Donna does, that their neediness contributed to their victimization. Popenoe points out that fatherless girls are also more vulnerable simply because they lack the protection of a second parent. A single mother, he points out, is likely to be stretched thinly over her responsibilities and less able to guard her child. And although some of the negative effects of fatherlessness may be countered by the presence of a surrogate father—a stepfather, an uncle, or even an older brother—such surrogates may also contribute to the problem. In his study, Popenoe states that nonbiological father figures are implicated in rising rates of child abuse, perhaps because of their lack of emotional involvement in children who are not genetically "their own." In Donna's case, her mother had remarried by the time of her rape, and her stepfather was not, as is sometimes the case, her attacker. But in

Donna's eyes, her new "dad" did not act like a father, either. As she recalls, her stepfather abdicated his responsibility to take care of his new family by failing to confront or accuse her attacker. "He had one chance to be my father and he blew it," she says, still angry nearly forty years later. Her stepfather was not the man she wanted, and the longing never abated.

"I looked a lot in my life for a dad," Donna says. "Most of my twenties were spent getting involved with married men who were a lot older than me. It's absolutely classic. At the time, I had no idea that that is what I was doing. It wasn't until my mid-thirties, when I was yet again involved with a married man, that I finally said, why are you doing this? Why are you doing this to yourself? This is nuts, this is crazy. Then when I looked back on all of my relationships, I realized that there was this self-destructive pattern. It really was my trying to replicate and live out the Oedipal fantasy. I was sleeping with Dad. Most of these men, not surprisingly, were a lot older than I. And the ones with whom I had the most passionate relationships were Irish. My father was Irish."

Even as she nears her fifties, Donna says, the compulsion remains with her. "I am still entranced by men in their sixties," she acknowledges with a little laughter. "Although, unfortunately, they are not so much older than me now. And a few years ago, I came very, very close to having an affair with a man who was seventy-two. That we didn't was his choice," she says, "and I regret it."

This "Daddy hunger" surfaces nearly across the board in women who lost their fathers as children. But the damage caused by this trauma plays out in different ways, largely according to our age at our parent's death. For example, an adolescent, who may be undertaking the developmental task of separating from her parents, may subliminally worry that her "rejection" of the family, her going off on her own, somehow contributed to the father's death. Logically, she will understand that this is not likely, but the repercussions of such a loss may trip her up as she makes her next steps out on her own as an adult. For her, the trauma may haunt her with guilt and mixed feelings about adult independence.

For younger children, as Turnbull points out, the problems can involve our most basic understanding of what death is. For death is a complex concept: the idea that someone will never again come home or tuck us in is profound, larger perhaps than most young children can comprehend. The loss is so painful and so complete that any reminder of it summons great terror. Add in that such an early loss deprives a young girl of many years of familiarity with their fathers, with men, with the "others" who play such a large role in our growth and development. Put these elements together, and it begins to makes sense that one of the most prevalent and lasting effects of the early loss of a father is fear—not fear of death specifically, but fear of men.

"When I was younger, I was definitely afraid of men," says Yael, echoing many other women who have reported vague fears about unknown and threatening males. She had a brother who was one year older, but a seven-year-old boy is not a man. And although their mother remarried once Yael was grown and out of the house, for many years the family lived in near isolation in the rural South, with little or no regular contact with adult men. To Yael, men were undeniably strange, large, and frankly terrifying. "I had nightmares about men," she says, recalling the terror that followed her into adulthood, and kept her awake at night after a career move to a big city. "I dreamed about men raping me, and I went through a period where I thought that they were a threat to me all the time."

Some of that fear may be due to unfamiliarity. But much of it seems to be a reaction to the great hurt these women felt when they lost their fathers. We all experience anger and abandonment when a loved one dies and leaves; how much more profound was that feeling of betrayal then for women who were too young to grasp what had happened? who had lost their fathers when they were only six or eight or ten years old? The lesson for such women, then, may be: if a father can die, perhaps no man can be trusted. In his study of eighty-one women, William S. Appleton saw the tracks of this fear in the way such women shied away from intimate relationships: "The daughters of the deceased," the Harvard psychiatrist wrote in *Fathers and Daughters*, "seem to shun symbiosis for fear of losing their mate as they did their father."

That distrust goes deep: "I have this weird feeling about guys," says Lilah, who lost her father to cancer when she was eleven. "I think maybe if my father hadn't died, I'd feel differently in regards to men. Because I feel like a lot of times it takes me a longer time to trust them."

This fear is well documented. E. Mavis Hetherington's landmark 1972 study of girls who had lost their fathers to divorce and to death remarked on it. Hetherington, a University of Virginia professor, set up interviews and then observed three separate groups each composed of twenty-four girls: girls from intact families, girls whose parents had divorced and were living with their mothers, and girls whose fathers had died. The seventy-two girls, who were from roughly the same social and economic backgrounds, ranged in age from thirteen to seventeen years old, and those who had lost their fathers had been bereaved anywhere from very early childhood through adolescence.

Hetherington used male and female researchers to interview the girls, and recorded their body language, including how far away from the researchers they sat, as well as the length and depth of their verbal responses. The results were striking. Daughters of widows, as Hetherington identifies them, smiled less at male questioners. They held themselves farther away from men and they talked less, giving shorter answers to all the questions. The younger the subject was at the time of her loss, the more extreme her reaction, with those who had lost their fathers before the age of five seeming to be the most profoundly affected. Overall, the girls whose fathers had died seemed more afraid of men than any of their peers. During a recreational dance, two of the girls actually hid in the bathroom for the entire evening. Hetherington proposed that these reactions demonstrated "apprehension and inadequate skills in relating to males."

Nearly every study of fatherless girls since has referred to this study, and the anecdotal evidence that has come up as I have spoken to women like Yael, Lilah, and Donna tends to confirm its findings. This early loss has shaped them, often leaving them scarred. However, it is crucial to remember that these women, like any of us, are not simply the sum of their injuries. As with so much of the trauma that we all experience, this early loss is just one factor, one aspect of our makeup. Like all the factors that feed into our lives, such fear and discomfort—or however we experience our early grief—must be seen as only one element in our lives, one part of our personality with which we must come to terms. It shapes us, but as adults we have some choices about how it plays into our lives. This early trauma may exaggerate other parts of our personality, our genetics and our environment, and its influence may be blown out of proportion. Or it may be worked through, with therapy or some alternative form of aided growth, and incorporated into the collage of who we are. It need not rule us. For women who have experienced such a loss, the resulting trauma may be seen as one very interesting piece of our personal puzzle.

To some women, this early trauma may help explain a particular sexuality: "I have always felt that my father's early death was one of a multitude of factors that has made it easier for me to love women then men," says Yael. Although she identifies herself as a lesbian, she describes feeling sexual attraction to men as well as women during her teen years.

"I was always very sexual," she says, describing her high-school dating years, during which she experimented with young men. "But although I became involved with men, I found myself just objectifying them pretty much, and not really trying very hard to bond with them. I was just not seeing them quite as human beings in the same way I see women. So, I think that for me, that when I figured out that you could actually have sex with women, and not just be friends and be close with them, and be intimate with them emotionally and mentally and every other way, I was just completely relieved."

Yael believes her sexuality springs from many sources, and may be genetically "hard wired" or predetermined. But the lingering effects of her childhood loss have certainly played a part in how she chooses to experience intimacy.

For other women, such as Donna, the family trauma allowed for a beneficial break in continuity. This gap may have allowed growth that would have been suppressed, she believes, had the family remained intact. "My mother and father were working-class. I have cousins, and I see my cousin Rebecca's life. Her father and my father were brothers. They were exactly the same social class. My life would have patterned hers. I absolutely broke out of the tradition. I am absolutely not in the class I was raised in. I would not have become a psychiatrist. In a very odd way, it gave me opportunities that I never would have had had my father lived."

While we tend to focus on the emotional effect of such a loss, in these cases of families with young children we also should look at its practical ramifications. For older daughters, bereaved as adults, economics is less of a factor. For young girls whose fathers die, economics can change everything. The death of a father, for example, often seriously alters a family's lifestyle and childcare situation. Widowed mothers, for example, may need to work outside the home, and are more likely to leave younger children with surrogate care. Single parent households, particularly those headed by women, are likely to have less money. Studies by the National Fatherhood Initiative reveal how families that have lost their male parent, either through death or the abandonment of the family, suffer in terms of resources. Families headed by women made up almost 49 percent, or nearly half, of the "poorest fifth" of all families, according to a U.S. Bureau of Census statistical abstract from 1997, and less than 1 percent of the wealthiest. Considering that gender equity for pay is still a long way off, this skewing of wealth away from women-run families seems likely to continue, even if it abates somewhat. And these changes may determine others, as when Lilah's mother moved her family from suburban Virginia back home to Chicago after her husband died. As with so many other changes, this one—made out of necessity—had a lasting impact on the young girl.

"I love the city," Lilah says now, more than fifteen years after the early loss that disrupted her family and her home. "I could still be in a fairly conservative small town. And then I might not have taken all the liberties in my life that I have. I might have stayed there, followed a different career choice. Everything could be different."

The loss of her father has shaped her in many ways, Lilah agrees. Perhaps it was the single most influential event of her childhood. She and Donna and Yael can all testify that such an early injury may have a great effect on who we grow to be. Now that we are adults, however, many of us have found ways to make peace with this trauma, to incorporate it into our adult lives. This truce is not without rewards.

As Donna explains, "The fact is, I have not had a 'relationship,'" she says, referring to the classic one-on-one intimacy of marriage or permanent cohabitation. "But I have been friends with this one guy for twenty years. We do everything together. We're certainly emotionally intimate with each other, but we're not physically intimate. We are just friends. You know, there are times when I look at that relationship and I think how much of that relationship is still protecting me from loss, from the loss of my father [by keeping me from finding a more comprehensive intimate relationship]. But I love having him in my life. It's a good relationship."

CHAPTER 4

Time for Mourning

G rief and the immediate impact of loss is affected by several factors, and in order to understand the changes we go through after our fathers are gone it is necessary to look at the means of their leavetaking. Our grief, our periods of mourning, and sometimes our ability to resolve issues brought up by our fathers' deaths may all be influenced by the various ways in which we lost them. We may lose them quickly, through accident, suicide, or sudden illness, or with more preparation and warning, as after a lingering illness. Equally important, we may find ourselves confronting, during our first mourning, our expectations of what such a life passage should be like, and the myriad ways our other family members respond. As all these factors play out in our mourning and the intensity of our grief, we may begin to discuss the resolution of father-daughter issues.

Perhaps in no way was I more my father's daughter than in the way I handled his dying. For starters, I wasn't there. I was at work. I had left the hospital shortly after noon to get to my job at the newspaper. I was assigned to the annual Christmas charity page, compiling the lists of donors and sizing the photos of proud business owners handing checks to a representative from the charity, usually some poor reporter dressed Santa-style in red suit and a white beard. Because of the beat, I was known that season as Santa's Elf, but I felt more dwarflike as I rushed into the charity's subterranean office each day to begin putting together the long lists of the generous and the good.

By the time my father had entered into the final phase of his illness, the holiday season had passed. The charity had a surplus of last-minute givers, however, and although we were no longer running the sob story appeals of little Jimmy who has never had a toy, or poor Susie, hospitalized after a nasty fall, we were still publishing the lists. The women I worked with, a clique of chain-smoking Irish-Catholic working moms who seemed light years away from my own Jewish, college-educated world, had some idea of my father's condition. They asked occasionally, and I would tell them I had visited him at the hospital. But although I certainly overheard their stories of family hardships often enough, I didn't feel a great sympathy there. *We're starting from too different places,* I told myself. *They think I'm a freak. I'm single at an age when most of their daughters are having their second or third babies. I'm not from the neighborhood. I don't smoke.* In truth, they probably didn't know what to make of the quiet copy editor who rushed down to their smoky den each afternoon and began typing furiously, as if to block out the sound of their chat or of any human outreach at all.

As luck would have it, they weren't there the day my father died. We were ending the fund drive for the year. The next day's section would be the last, and by the time I got to the paper the women had already added up the final notices of funds and donors. I arrived to an empty office; the door was propped open—strictly against policy—and a note tacked to it told me to file quickly and join the party at the Harp and Bard around the corner. My father had been unconscious when I'd left him. When I'd shown up for my lunchtime visit, after completing the morning job that I held at Harvard, he'd been lying there as if asleep, his face twitching and lips moving as if he were dreaming. He'd often been asleep when I'd visited, increasingly so as the ratio of morphine and cancer to life had tipped him toward the inevitable. But that day he'd looked clearly different, his once ruddy face particularly yellow, his hands beginning to draw up, like a dog's begging paws, or like a fetus's. I'd met my mother there, as was our custom, and, as had also become customary, I hadn't known what to say. I believe she said, "He's going," but all I remember clearly is the way he looked all waxy and fake and that my own head felt fuzzy and full of noise. I know I kissed him on his cool cheek because I remember feeling somewhat afraid. *Was this it?* I know I didn't stay long. Although the afternoon job was ending, and my future at the paper was uncertain, I was glad to have that office to go to for one more day.

I was not in the mood for the party that would be filling the backroom of the nearby bar with bad jokes and more smoke. I was not, really, in the mood to work. I logged on and checked my electronic messages. "We're at the Harp. Don't forget the three photos—top desk drawer. Screw these up and you're out. And lock the goddamned door!" The ill-natured message from the chief Santa, a semiretired, more than semialcoholic old reporter, sounded just like his other daily forays had, grumpy and profane in a rather jovial fashion. I wished he were there to grumble and curse in person. He would, at least, have gotten me started. As it was I located the last photos and stared at them. Not having the energy to measure and mark them for the next day's page, I called my home number to check for phone messages. There were two from my mother. "Please call me when you get this," the first said. There seemed to be something in her throat. I didn't need the second to tell me that my father was dead, although that one told me where she was—at a funeral home near the hospital—and how to reach her.

I hesitated before I called her back. She hadn't known I'd picked up the message. I started to work on that day's totals, gathering into one long file all of the short lists of numbers that the women had typed into the system, and formatting them to appear in print. Unable to concentrate, I found my totals not adding up, and realized that I'd cut and pasted one list in twice. I moved to take it out and cut out too much. "Shit," I said, to no one in particular. The room was dark, one high window the only opening to the winter afternoon. My throat itched from the smoke that would probably never completely clear. I called my parent's home and heard my father's voice on the answering machine. "This is the Simon household." I hung up, and called the funeral home. An anonymous man with the soft voice of professional comfort assured me that he would connect me and a moment later I was talking to my mother. "This was for the best," she said. "I'll be there within the hour," I told her. I wanted her to say she'd taken care of everything, that I should stay at work. She didn't, and instead I jotted down directions and hung up, trying to make sense out of the blinking green figures on the screen before me.

I know I made it to the funeral home not long after. I know that before I left I found the presence of mind to call the night editor and explain the situation, and that she immediately took over, telling me not to worry as she shooed me off the phone. I believe I can still recall the dim, quiet office where I found my mother listening as a strange man in a suit talked about the one-day waiting period that was necessary before a cremation. But I don't know how I got there, or really where these memories come from, for I could also swear to this day that none of this really happened. These flashes are just that, as unreal as any dream.

If we follow the classic outline first proposed by Elisabeth Kubler-Ross and allow for our reaction to death to follow the stages set forth for dying, then denial is the first stage of grief. When something so painful happens, we want so desperately for it to not be true that we will ourselves to believe that it isn't—that it hasn't happened at all. Our age, our relative maturity has little impact on the force of this grief, which is primal, as basic as our own will toward life. The fact that in the natural order we are supposed to survive our parents does little to mitigate the depth of this loss or the intensity of our reaction. If anything, the assumption that such a loss is normal and natural, is at any rate preferable to the alternative of parents mourning their children, makes getting past our denial a little harder. We fear our pain; we fear being thought "childish" in the eyes of our colleagues and friends. And so we suppress our reactions.

"I'm just . . . surprised, that's all. It's so sudden." I remember my mother saying when we heard that her father, my grandfather, had died of a massive coronary and the subsequent wreck of the car he'd been driving. She was daubing at the tears welling up in her eyes as she talked to me, and it is quite possible that she sobbed in private, away from her youngest child. In public, however, she was very calm, very what I thought of as "adult." That was nearly thirty years ago, but I remember the look in her eyes, the handkerchief—probably my father's—balled up in her hand, with one corner peeking out for use. I assume I recall it so clearly because I had been shaken at the sight of my mother crying; at the time, I didn't think of the daughter who had just lost her father.

Feeling the Loss

Many of us report weeks, and even months, spent working through the stages defined by Kubler-Ross, from denial and isolation, through anger, bargaining, and depression before eventually reaching the peace of acceptance. Nora still recalls the great anger she felt at her father, how furious she felt toward him for dying before she could reach his hospital bed. She wanted to say goodbye, but the two-hour drive to her hometown was too long for him to hold out, and she still can remember how her panic turned to hot rage when she heard, on her arrival at the hospital, that he was already gone. We bargain by being the caregivers, half allowing ourselves to believe that if we are just very, *very* good girls, this time things will work out. And when they don't, we react, often badly: Nella remembers the weeks of grim depression, when getting out of bed seemed pointless and way too strenuous. Two years after her father's death, Anna is only now able to think about returning to work, and the mountains of bills and legal problems that her time off entailed have not served to make her return to the land of the living any easier. We get stuck in these passages toward acceptance, toward resolution; sometimes we need to take longer than others do, or than others understand.

As this transition makes clear, no matter how old we are the parent-child relationship retains its potency. No matter what our age, when our fathers die we are losing Daddy. "As an adult, when you lose a parent, you're losing your mommy, you're losing your daddy. You regress," explains Carol Tosone, an associate professor of social work at New York University who has worked for many years with families in the grieving process.

This is a step back we daughters know well. While the societal basis for our behavior may be murky, our reactions aren't. The evidence of our actions is clear: It is we daughters, rather than our brothers, who react most strongly to this primal prompt. According to the observations of those who work closely with bereaved families, it is uniformly daughters who attend bedside vigils, who make the most regular visits during the final days or weeks or months. It is the daughters who appear more openly upset, the most wounded by the oncoming loss.

We daughters seem to feel this loss more strongly than others in our families do. We, more than our brothers, have remained attached to our parents as adults, and it is overwhelmingly daughters, professionals note, who attend to them in their final stages. "The caregivers are always the daughters," confirms Barbara Gilfoyle, a social worker and the director of bereavement services for

Calvary Hospital in New York, who lost her own father several years ago. And although this role may fit societal expectations—sons, the stereotype goes, are more involved with the new families they have created—what is surprising is that for many of us the final vigil beside our fathers is often more difficult than the same vigil would be by the bedside of our mothers. Despite our closeness to our mothers, despite our bone-deep sadness at their loss, experts such as Gilfoyle report, we may be more disoriented by the death of our fathers. "One of the questions that I've always asked people who are intimately involved with a patient is, 'What do you see your life being like after the death of the patient?' And in several of the cases with fathers and daughters, the daughter was unable to say what her life was going to be like. She had no idea," says Gilfoyle, still saddened. "I don't see this with daughters and mothers."

Some of this may be attributed to the combined weight of our traditional roles. As the daughters, we are the ones expected to be the caregivers. As women, we are expected to maintain relationships, an additional burden that we may not feel with our mothers, who may—even on their own deathbeds—be expected to play a bonding or hostess role in family interactions. With these dual expectations, we feel coerced to sit by the bedside in the hospice, to be the ones who call and comfort and visit. We are the children who have believed that it is expected of us that we fit our lives to our families. While caring for our fathers, we often voluntarily limited our lives for them, and thus we find ourselves surprised when our lives do go on after theirs have ended.

"I just never imagined my life without my father," recalls Shayna, whose adored father died two years ago of pancreatic cancer. "And what bothered me the most was that there was this profound alteration in my view of the world after he died. But my day-to-day life didn't change. How come? Why didn't his death affect everything?"

Expected or Surprised

The common mythology of grief holds that to lose someone suddenly is more traumatic than to watch a dear one slowly waste away. The shock, bewilderment, and disbelief that always accompany death, writes Edward Myers in *When Parents Die*, is usually intensified when the loss is unexpected. Plus, an unanticipated loss, the conventional wisdom runs, allows less time for resolution of old issues and less time to prepare for the inevitable.

Certainly, unexpected death carries a greater element of surprise, a greater dislocation of expectation and routine than a death coming at the end of a long illness. The disorientation it can cause may have reverberations throughout our practical lives, for example if settling insurance concerns or other household finances had been postponed. It may also fracture our faith in what we had deemed certainties; if someone we love who has seemed hale and strong suddenly ceases to exist we may proceed for some time on tenterhooks, always expecting our world to be turned upside-down again, and it may be a long while before we learn to trust once more. Those of us who have lost our fathers without warning, particularly if they were young and otherwise healthy-seeming men, report that shock is usually the first and clearest aspect of our grief. The loss of certainty and trust follows close behind.

"When he died, it was instantaneous," says Rosie, whose father was only sixty-three when he suffered a heart attack in front of his daughter, wife, and son-in-law. In retrospect, Rosie views this kind of death as a mixed blessing. She believes this was the way he would have wanted to go. A vibrant, athletic man, her father would not have tolerated illness or a slow decline, she says. "My father could never have suffered through a long illness. He couldn't have done it. He was strong and healthy and to have him languish in a nursing home or hospital—I can't even imagine it."

At the same time," she continues, such a loss took a greater toll on her and her family than a lingering death in a hospital. "I think those hospital experiences give loved ones the opportunity to internalize it and deal with it," she says. "Whereas if somebody dies instantly right in front of you, one minute they're there and the next minute, they are absolutely gone. That sort of instantaneous departure leaves me with this hole, wondering, you know, where is he? what happened?" Despite her sense of acceptance, seen in her belief that her father's death was the "right" death for him, the shock lingers.

To further complicate the grieving process, if the death is caused by unnatural means—through suicide or homicide—the normal quotients of fear and guilt that always accompany a loss are ratcheted up enormously. We wonder: Should we have seen warning signs? Was there anything we could have done to intervene? The cost of such a death to the entire family is enormous, and may disrupt our domestic patterns indefinitely.

"I felt responsible in the sense of 'Could I have stopped this?' " recalls Tina, a psychotherapist whose father killed himself close to thirty years ago. She recalls feeling particularly alienated from her friends because of the nature of her father's death, her loss aggravated both by shock and the family's sense of shame. "For me, it brought up issues of trust and safety. Specifically, for a long time, I feared I was dangerous. That in loving any man, I had the capacity to hurt him, to drain him. For a long time it was hard for me to see that what was inside them wasn't of my making."

Even when the cause of death is natural, we often hear about the lack of resolution that accompanies an unexpected death, stories, for example, of the last squabble in an otherwise friendly relationship, or the final, unhappy visit. The theory runs that those whose fathers pass away at the end of a long decline will have had a chance to stage manage a more benign farewell.

Such a fast farewell, however, may not be all bad. Although the effects of shock and sometimes shame or guilt that may accompany an unexpected death cannot be discounted, it is important to keep in mind that there are complicating factors in every leavetaking. Clearly the people who refer to a slow decline as preferable are discounting the wear and tear of long-term illness, the tensions that pile up as the patient declines and the family's normal interactions (and sometimes professional and financial obligations as well) are put on indefinite hold. They are not counting the cost in days and nights spent in hospitals and hospices, away from our own jobs and mates and children. They are not counting the stress of what experts call anticipatory grieving, a nagging and draining ache that is increased not only by the fear of what is to come but also by our guilt over our preoccupation with the coming end.

Yes, it is true there is more time in cases like mine. There is undoubtedly less surprise in the death of fathers who were elderly or had been suffering for a long time. But sometimes the resources we have when a dear one is dying seem to be predetermined and roughly equal. What those who lose someone suddenly suffer due to the unexpected nature of their loss, the rest of us have taken from us by immense fatigue. We are never really ready for someone to die. As social worker Barbara Gilfoyle puts it: "Death is *always* a shock. No matter how incapacitated the person was, he was there before. Now he's gone."

True, unlike an unexpected death, a long fatal illness offers the opportunity for settling old scores. But the chance for a deathbed resolution, particularly when the dying person is a father, runs counter to too many factors of the relationship to be of much help to the survivor, particularly to us daughters. What I experienced, the stasis of long-term suffering, is more common. Many of us had time, for sure, but too often we found ourselves frozen throughout the last weeks or months by the pain and by our past, particularly by the unacknowledged shifting of roles as we watched our strong daddies become weak. Too often our fathers encourage this rigidity. Still clinging to the images of themselves as the big men who took care of us, they are reluctant to relinquish control in the sight of their little girls.

I know my father hated the physical weakness that accompanied his slow dying, hated my seeing him as vulnerable, as less strong and physically competent then he once had been. I recall how he detested his own decline, how he struggled against the loss of control over his own life, and perhaps also over mine. For I remember how he dismissed me, when I first raced to the hospital in answer to my mother's anguished call, four weeks before that final afternoon.

"Your father's been taken to the emergency room." I remember her saying. I don't believe I heard anything else. I had been at my morning job when the call had come through, and I had yelled a quick word to my supervisor and torn out of there. I didn't think to do otherwise. My mother, certainly, was glad I had come, when I found her in the waiting area of the emergency room, where she had been alternately pacing and sitting, trying to pass the time since the ambulance she had called had arrived and her husband of forty-seven years been whisked away.

It was my father, groggy and surly, who wished me gone, when some long minutes later we were escorted in to see him in his curtained alcove, his chin still dirty with the charcoal they had forced into him to neutralize the painkillers he had swallowed in quantity in his attempt to once and for all finally kill his pain.

"What are you doing here?" At first he was too out of it to put together another sentence and his head fell back, his eyes closed. But when he could finally focus on me he again questioned my presence. "Why are you here? You should be at work. Go back to work," he commanded me weakly.

"She wanted to be with you," my mother explained as I, at a loss for words, stood staring stupidly at my prone and broken father. "We both did. We love you." He sighed, with resignation or fatigue, and closed his eyes again. Someone in a white coat came to tell us that he would be admitted, but that he seemed now to be in a stable condition. More attendants came in, and he roused a bit, enough to murmur to my mother. Enough, I still hope, to indicate that he understood why she had called 911 when she came home to find him unconscious and barely breathing. He seemed to have used up his energy for me, however, and although he reached up to weakly pat my check when I bent to kiss him, I knew I had been dismissed. My mother had interrupted his private drama, but she had at least been part of the long, painful nights and the drifting days. I was an intruder on his dignity. He was probably unconscious again as they wheeled him out into the hallway, but as he went by me I told him I was returning to the office, which I did, and which I continued to do throughout the weeks remaining in his dying.

My father grew fond again in those last weeks, but he never truly grew comfortable with the exposure of his vulnerability to me. His best days were those in which he was oblivious, distracted by his remaining pleasures or his pride in me. And although I looked warily for openings during which I could nurse him a bit, or at least express my solicitude, I never really found any. As the days passed, I began to hope less ardently for such opportunities; in fact, contrary to my expectations, his silence grew to be what I desired as well. His discomfort had ratcheted up the volume on my own dread, just as my uneasiness probably illustrated all too clearly to him the inevitable conclusion to his hospitalization. I waited with increasing edginess for a way to make a gracious shift in our roles, and every day went home a little relieved that none had been made.

My story doesn't illustrate the only way for such endings to play out. In a healthy relationship, where such roles are more flexible, a daughter and her father may be better able to cope with these changes. Some women do talk about the fulfillment of being able to give back, to care for a father as they were themselves once cared for, sometimes at the expense of their own lives.

"My dad got sick in November, and in February I applied for a really great job, but I knew it wasn't going to happen," recalls Keri. "I felt like I needed to be available for my parents." Because of her commitment to them, and perhaps her lack of focus on her own goals at that time, she didn't get the job. Such a decision was not entirely hers to make, but her ambivalence certainly helped tip the scale. She was going through the motions toward getting a new job, but what she really wanted to do was nurse her father, a choice many of us still at least consider.

We don't always have the option. The sad paradox in all of this is that, although our fathers are the parents more likely to age faster and need our help sooner, the barriers to our giving that help are the highest to overcome. By the time we are adults, we have probably seen our mothers cry. We may have sat with them, even sympathized over a slight or a cruelty from our fathers. Particularly if we were the daughters of divorce, we may have sided with our mothers and learned to see them in a sisterly way. Although we may have had problems respecting our mothers, we didn't revere them in the way we did our fathers. For good or ill, our fathers were usually the ones with power, and to see them sick or disabled shakes us up. For these men to be able to share their weaknesses with their daughters is often harder still. Aging, as many of us already know, is not easy. And despite the excellent example presented by sister Beth of *Little Women*, illness seldom brings out the best in us. Thus perhaps it is unfair to expect our fathers (who may never have read Louisa May Alcott at all) to act nobly in such extremes.

What is more likely, and perhaps more common, is reversion. At best, our fathers tend to flip back into the modes that long worked for them, often hanging on to the mode of omniscient daddy long past the point when such power has clearly become illusory. At times, we even help them maintain this illusion: "When my sister called, saying it seemed serious, I booked a flight for the next day," says Vicky. "But I was actually worried about how it would it appear. What would he think if I was so worried about him?"

At worst, our fathers act as most of us do when faced with pain, with sickness, and with fear. They may become cranky and uncommunicative, out of discomfort and unhappiness. Not wanting to face the reality of their fates, the inevitable end that they see reflected in our grief and fear, they may become hostile or sullen to chase us—their clearest mirrors—away. They become, in other words, childish and scared and irrational, even less the parents we want, just when we may be needing them to rise to the challenge of fatherhood one final time.

Making Peace

Some of the happiest women I have spoken with are the ones whose fathers, despite their failings, managed to leave gracefully. Greta, whose father died suddenly of a massive heart attack, found her healing eased by the memories of her final conversation with him. She remembers laughing with him, and a fond hug for a farewell, although neither knew that it would be the last at the time.

"My father died early in December; the last time I saw him was at Thanksgiving," she recalls. "And he had a new car and I remember him dropping me off to get picked up by the airport limousine shuttle and we couldn't open the door. I remember laughing. And I remember when I got the call that he had died, afterward, it was sort of okay because we were laughing the last time I saw him. I mean, he was happy with me."

That final memory, rather than the suddenness of his death, is what has stayed with her. Indeed, the unexpected nature of his death—he had collapsed on a golf course—may have made such a gracious leavetaking possible, or at least more likely.

In the opposite case, when a dying father is unable to accept the changing levels of competence despite the evidence of physical frailty, the discrepancy (the open secret of his failing health) places another burden on top of our growing worry and impending grief. In such cases, as happened with my father, they are abdicating what may be the final duty of a parent, to let us be the adults, to let us finally assume the caregiver role as they prepare to leave us.

Indeed, the best indication of how we will grieve and recover from our loss may not lie in how our fathers die, but in how we dealt with them living. And for those of us who were unable to make peace with our fathers during their lifetimes, our way to peace and to healing may lie in accepting this lack of resolution, accepting our own and our fathers' flaws. Even if our fathers cannot at this final crisis abandon their illusions about their role, and our relationship, we must. For only by letting go of the fantasy of the perfect daddy, and of the perfect deathbed reconciliation, can we achieve anything resembling closure.

Laying down our illusions during this one last test can be extremely difficult. I recall with great pain the times that I tried to communicate with my father during those last few weeks. I remember telling him that he need not worry about me, despite my history of jumping from one bad romance into another. I had known how pained he always was, when I'd been unable to hide my tears or they'd caught me moping around after some handsome jerk had given me the heave-ho. And I had wanted him to know that at some level, I too had known these men weren't worth crying over. In the solemnity of his final hospitalization, in the new, clear perspective that his dying had given me, I knew quite plainly that I had often made my little dramas into big ones. I knew that for some reason I had been spinning my wheels. As he lay dying, I wanted to share with him my new awareness; I wanted him to know that I wasn't the truly helpless romantic that I often appeared to be, and that there was a smart and self-preservative woman under all the mawkish sentimentality. I wanted him to know that I was working it out and that, at some point, I would be all right.

The awkward silence that followed my attempts at broaching the subject nearly closed me down completely. We had never talked much about relationships, certainly not about sex or romance, and now our mutual embarrassment had reached flood level. I didn't know how to relieve the pressure. *I just want you to know, I never believed I was going to marry Bruce*, I remember saying. *I knew I was just taking it all way too seriously*. I tried again: *I don't want you to worry that I don't know when it's not right like that.*

My words made little sense and his lack of response didn't add to their coherence. He was stony, cold, and clearly uncomfortable with what I was saying. I tried again the next day, and got a similar response. Finally, I told him, "I just wanted you to know," and left it at that. Since then, I've realized that it wasn't my father's peace I was trying to assure, but my own. That in the final hours I wanted to make up for all the years that we had never talked about such things, and that to do so now was impossible.

For Marcy, whose father was always a stern and distant figure, this kind of silence added a layer of grief she could not have anticipated. "I have the sadness and the disappointment of not having more of a relationship with my father," she begins. "And I have the sadness of not being able to tell him during his illness how I felt and that he had been my hero as a child."

Marcy and I are not alone; particularly between daughters and fathers such barriers are common. This does not make them any less tragic: "I was visiting with him and he had said to me—I'm the oldest of five children—that he wanted to talk with me about finances," says Lillian, whose father died of a rare bone cancer four years ago. "Each time I was going to see him there I kept trying to gear myself up to talk to him about feelings, talk to him about how we felt about all of this. What did he feel, were there things he wanted to say? I wanted to talk to him about what he was going through and what he was facing. We got as far as having that one conversation, him saying that he wanted to talk to me about finances, that he felt I was the one that he could best talk to about all of that. I said, 'Of course.' When I came back two weeks later, he was no longer capable of having that conversation."

Release and Relief

Despite such great and overriding sadness, those of us whose parents were older or ill often speak of the release of death. Especially for those of us who saw our fathers' lives reduced through weakness or the daily humiliations that accompany diseases like Alzheimer's, we may have longed for the relief that death would bring. The cessation of pain and fear become a positive, a longed-for conclusion. When it came, however, it usually brought an accompanying load of guilt and shame. It is difficult to admit that there is an element of good mingled in with all the hurt and confu-

sion, with the utter dislocation that death brings, and that makes
the mixture harder to bear. But swallowing such a mixture is possible, although it is rarely simple or easy. Sometimes the only way to
come to terms with such a sought-after death is by acknowledging
its bittersweet nature and our own conflicted longing.

"I think the way they died was a big factor in the grief I felt,"
recalls Wendy, whose father lingered, ill, for months, and whose
mother died much more quickly several years later. "I don't think
it's easier, one way or the other. My dad was sick for a long time,
and we knew that he was going to die. It was a torturous time for
the whole family, and when it finally happened, we were relieved
that he no longer had to suffer. A lot of people don't understand
that until they have experienced it themselves. We didn't *want* him
to die, but we wanted him to be free of any more pain. I felt a lot
of guilt for wanting him to go, and thought it was selfish of me,
that I did not want to have to deal with it anymore. The combination of emotions is excruciating."

Sometimes, the beneficence of death is just what it appears: an
end of suffering, an end of the degradation and shame of increasing enfeeblement, an end of otherwise unlimited pain. However,
the relief that often accompanies death may also come from our
conflicts. Precisely because some of our issues seemed irreconcil-
able, death may mean an end to fighting, to fear, and to the constant disappointment of relating to a parent who will never, in any
stretch of time, accept us for who we are. Writing about the nature
of grief and bereavement in *When Parents Die,* Edward Myers talks
about this reaction, calling it "appropriate" and saying "You may
end up feeling . . . relief that you are now spared further effort,
emotional upheaval, and family conflict." However, with the end
of active conflict also comes the end of any possibility for reconciliation. In families such as ours, that loss must be mourned as well,
with as much peace and dignity as possible.

"When he was dying, at first I tried to speed up our level of
intimacy to fill in all the pieces before he died," says Nora whose
father also died of prostate cancer, about a year before mine. By

the time Nora's father's months of aches and pains were correctly diagnosed, his cancer had already metastasized throughout his body and he wasn't given long to live. But the weeks turned to months, and through the process Nora found herself relaxing into the process. Although she never achieved the ease and openness she wanted with her hard-driving parent, a recovering alcoholic, she did find in herself a certain acceptance for the man he was, and for the way he had always treated her.

"Toward the end of his death, I began to realize that I was never going to fill in the gaps and change the relationship. I had to accept it for exactly what it was in the present. I think, with time, he and I may have come to a closer relationship, but that time was not there. Being able to let go and take him and our relationship as it was, was very freeing. I think overall in my life it has relaxed me. I am sure that I am better able to accept my close relationships for what they are, to know that not being able to change that can be okay."

Facing the Pain

Whatever resolution we can find in death—and many prefer the term "resignation" to the Kubler-Ross ideal of "acceptance"—we cannot downplay its effect. We cannot allow ourselves to be prematurely comforted, for such comfort is false, and ends up prolonging our pain and mourning.

Unfortunately, this stoic quality, this willful need for the pain, often brings us into conflict with the friends and loved ones to whom we look for support. I know that in the first weeks of mourning, I did not want to hear about "relief," about any "blessed conclusion." Yet those were the phrases that seemed to recur over and over in the brief and stilted conversations with my friends and colleagues in that first period following my father's death. Those who stressed such a happy ending on me did so primarily because of their own discomfort with death, I now believe.

It's their easy way out. They want to say something, they know they should, and yet they are either stymied by the rawness of our grief or too terrified of such evidence of mortality to face what has happened. And so they seek the equivalent of a happy ending: this death is a *good* thing. They look to us to confirm this sunny resolution, perhaps to allay their own fears. Often they mean well, and often they have had no experience of their own with such a crisis. In friends who have otherwise been true, such callousness is forgivable, but it's never easy.

Perri, for example, tries to explain her boyfriend's apparent indifference because she wants to stay with him and she needs a way to understand how insensitive he has been. She tells me, perhaps with some accuracy, that she thinks that his reaction can be blamed in part on his age (he is in his early twenties) and partly on herself, on the dominant role she had assumed in their relationship. She had always been the more competent, active one, and now, she believes, she is paying the price for not insisting on a more equal arrangement.

"In general, I am the type of person who reacts really well in emergency situations and he knows that," says Perri, a young nursing student who found herself battling crippling depression in the two years since her father's death. "Right after my dad died, although I had never been through it before, I knew exactly what to do. Four hours after he was dead, we were making a list of everybody we needed to call. We had life insurance policies; we had everything down. And, I thought that that would mean that I was really going to handle this well. But two weeks after he was dead I was in bed. I mean, I didn't get out of bed for the longest time, except to go to work, and I don't think my boyfriend could understand that."

Only after months of inactivity could she begin to pull herself together. "Part of it," she concedes now, "was that nobody wanted to talk about it with me." Although she and her boyfriend had been together for four years, he could not understand what she was going through. He actively discouraged her attempts to express her grief. "He would tell me the more you talk about it the less likely you are to get over it," she recalls. Although she is still working on their relationship, it is clear that she is much more aware of her own needs now. Chief among those is her need to express her sadness and live—for awhile—with the raw, wailing quality of her loss. What she needs is acceptance, not false comfort.

Grief

Although peace may be possible, however our fathers lived or died, grief is unavoidable. Whatever our emotions are at this change in our families and our own lives, our expression of them in some way is necessary. They are the means by which we process a profound and permanent loss. Whatever form our grief takes— depression, outright sadness, feelings of insecurity, and reappraisal of the solidity of the world around us—we are, for a little while, its servant, and those of us who chose to disregard our need to mourn only end up postponing the inevitable. Living, as we do, in a culture that embraces competence, we may find this truth running counter to our usual and expected can-do attitude.

Nella puts it best: "In my family," she says, "you deal with crises. You clean up the mess, you clear up the broken glass, and then you go into the other room to throw up." Perhaps if Nella had followed through with her own prescription she would have had an easier time after her father died. After all, she was the one who found him on the floor after his second stroke, after a strange prescience urged her to open her parents' bedroom door. And she was the one who sat by his bed for his final three days, holding his hand. But she, like so many of us, then put off the accompanying flood of feeling, trying instead to return to routine without the break her shock and sadness required. For Nella, as with me, the norm seemed both comforting and unattainable in the months afterward. In her case, the grief she refused to express surfaced in the form of suicidal thoughts that kept her confined to her bed for many days. Her father had pressed for her to finish her college degree and she desperately wanted to, but the black voices of her unexpressed emotions nearly sabotaged all her hard work. Only through an extreme effort of will did she manage to graduate, six months behind her original class. But that effort cost her the last of her denial: The day after she received her diploma, all the sadness and fear, the shock of finding him lying so still, and the wait by his bedside, caved in on her. "I sobbed for hours," she now recalls. "I just could not stop crying." Her time for mourning had come.

Not all of us can face this pain, not right away, but the sad fact is that we must. When not exposed to the air and the light, such strong feelings grow toxic, forming blisters of poison inside of us. If we are lucky, we eventually acknowledge and drain them. Some would say that the rituals of various religions and cultures exist to help us do so. Many Jewish women have told me of the "fresh" sadness they have felt when their fathers' grave sites were marked on the first anniversary of the death. Lapsed Catholics talk of returning to church, of requesting masses to mark the passing of parents who had held on to the religious formalities—another illustration of how a tradition can help tap into and acknowledge grief. Some women who do not follow a formal religion have told me they found it helpful to create their own ceremonies, perhaps choosing to gather family members on the deceased's birthday, for example, or to dedicate an anniversary day to doing charitable work in a lost parent's name. Many women have talked to me of such rituals and of familial triumphs that their fathers never got to see—the unknown grandson's first hockey game, the bat mitzvah or first communion—and the new tears they bring. Such tears can be good things; they are the milestones of mourning that we must pass if we are to move on to anything resembling peace.

Even if we can never truly work our minds around to acceptance, we may as well resign ourselves to grieving. For like death, grief is inevitable. We have the choice of *when* we deal with it but not *if*, because unresolved grief doesn't lessen. In the process of interviewing women for this book, I got a startling lesson in this as again and again I found women who had not let themselves mourn, who had deep pockets of unresolved grief. Granted, I was asking about painful times, and the women talking to me were dredging up memories of great sadness. But for many of them, years and even decades beyond the loss, the sadness seemed unabated. Sentences went unfinished, sobbing was audible over long-distance phone lines. Once more, the issue of self-selection raised its head: The women who agreed to talk with me were probably those who, like myself, were still bound up somehow in their fathers' death. But for these women the wounds were still raw, as sharp and deep as if the news had just come with my call. They had not let the pain out before; now, years later, it came up raging.

For such women, the freshness of grief is acute, as real as it was on the day of the loss. Its pain is fresh, no matter how long ago the death occurred. For unresolved mourners, as social worker Carol Tosone puts it, "it's almost like the loss becomes encapsulated, so time can go by but it doesn't change it." At its most extreme, when we hold this grief inside ourselves, we also mummify other aspects of our lives—sometimes literally, keeping old objects or even entire rooms unchanged because they remind us of the dead. More commonly, however, we simply freeze our own hearts. What is too painful to deal with is locked away. But such grief does not heal. When tapped—and it will be by a memory, an incident, or the mention of a shared joy—it will spring forth as hurtful as the day it was first received. Only when it is finally confronted, with sobs and anger or days in bed, can it begin to lessen. For mourning of this sort may take years, but it does mellow. Happiness and energy return, given time and courage.

Our fathers' dying, that last act, is finite and limited by time. It is strange to think that something with such a permanent effect on us belongs to only one point in time. But despite its permanence, the actual loss does belong to just one time. It happens, and then it is over, and we must remember and be grateful for that. He will be gone from us, at least in this life, forever. But the event, the horrible moment of loss, is finite. Once it has happened, we begin the process of mourning. And if we let ourselves experience our grief and confusion in the natural order, then we can heal. We can move on, and given time and any opportunity to express the often conflicting mass of emotions within us, we will.

No matter how difficult our grief is, those of us who have lost our fathers to death may still be in a better position to heal than those whose fathers disappeared from our lives because of ongoing chronic illness, such as Alzheimer's or severe mental illnesses, or because they abandoned us. Whereas we may feel burdened by the finality of our loss, we are also released by it. As explorations into the stress of ongoing grief by psychiatric professionals such as Pauline Boss have shown, the awful pressure of waiting, of not knowing, with its lure of false hope, can be worse than knowing. As Elyce Wakerman writes in *Father Loss*, women whose fathers are absent but not dead exist in a neverland of waiting, haunted by "the possibility of reconciliation." As Hetherington's studies of young girls make clear, the effect of such unresolved loss is haunting: girls whose fathers are dead may be shy of strangers. They may avoid men because they associate men with loss and pain, and because they know that their protective father no longer exists. Girls whose fathers have left the family through divorce or abandonment, on the other hand, tend to be more outgoing—but in a needy, desperate way that often increases at puberty. They feel as if they might be able to regain what has been lost if only they can find the key, the behavior, the right damn thing to say, and when they do not win back the lost parent, they feel responsible. Nor is it easy for them to find peace, for there is always one more trick to try. As any of us who have experienced the death of a chronically ill loved one recognizes, this extended mourning saps strength as it appears to grant hope. For girls still finding themselves, it is an incredible burden with which to live. For women, even those of us who have found our ways, it may still be the paradigmatic fate worse than death.

Choosing Life

Perhaps in this light, we may also begin to consider the benefits of death. For one effect of the death of a loved one is the renewed gusto it gives us for life. When someone close to us dies, we are forced to witness the fragility of life, its brevity and frailty. We see how close we all are to the end, how narrow, finally, that border is. And while that frailty terrifies us—and may traumatize many of us for quite a while to come—it often also makes life all the more dear. Call it the "carpe diem" reaction, the realization that because our days are numbered, they—and the opportunities inherent within—must be seized, must be treasured. Coming out of the chrysalis of mourning, we may be flooded with energy. We may find ourselves able to attack our projects with renewed enthusiasm and discard those things and people that we have previously allowed to drain us. We may fall in love anew with life.

"Right after my dad died, I quit my job," says Georgia, laughing. "His death really made me realize that you are not here forever and you really have to be happy with what you are doing. So, I think that helped me leave my job and try to find something that I would be more happy with. And, nine months or so after he died, my boyfriend and I ended up getting engaged. We had been living together for several years, and pretty happy with things, but after Dad died I realized I did want to move on. I wanted to buy a house; I wanted to get married; I wanted to do all those things and I didn't want to wait forever."

"Now I want to live," said Nina, when I first asked her if her goals had changed since the sudden collapse and death of her father six months before. "As in stop-and-smell-the-roses live. Instead of just taking life, which is what I've always done. I mean, I got good grades because I was bright. I got a nice car because I was clever with the numbers and I made the payments work. But I never really *wanted* things. Now I want my son to learn his ABCs; I want to get my house painted. I want to plant flowers."

For Nina, still in the first stages of mourning, this new appreciation of life is a tribute to her father. "I want to quit sitting around and worrying about 'do you remember when he did this or do you remember when he did that?' " she explains. "I want to go out and find him in today." For Lillian, several years past her initial crisis, it provides a continuous spur toward the simple joys of her life. "Life is precious, and it goes," she says succinctly. "And so I'm trying to keep thinking of things I want to do. Carving out time for my friends. Trying to walk as much as I can. Having an intellectual life. I want more in my life than just survival."

Across the board in our personal and professional lives, I witnessed this effect as part of our mourning process, perhaps the final stage as we awaken from our grief and choose to rededicate ourselves to life. Some women, like me, take a pragmatic approach. We see in this loss and the accompanying elation a natural economy. What we learn may be scarce becomes more valuable. For others, this gusto takes on a spiritual or religious aspect, and some chose to view it as a gift from their departed fathers. "It was a spiritual deepening," says Kim. "Being with my father while he was dying was the most alive I have felt since I gave birth."

No matter to whom or to what we attribute it, the lesson comes: Life is dear. And however we choose to experience this beautiful commodity—whether it be through work or art, lovers or children—we do so with renewed zest. To some extent, this factor may be the initial motivation for the majority of changes I have witnessed in the women in this book. It may have provided the spark. What we must look at next, however, is how that spark catches, and in what ways we use its energy. The death of our fathers frees us from some of our old ways of life and inspires us to grow in others. What we do next is up to us.

CHAPTER 5

Connecting with a Mate

As my own experience proved, one of the clearest and yet most confusing trends is that of single women suddenly committing to serious relationships in the years immediately following the death of our fathers. To get at the reasons behind this mass movement into commitment, we must examine how this loss influences both who we choose and how we conduct ourselves in relationships. Digging deeper, we can explore our changes in expectations and the evolution of some of our fears, dreams, and perceptions.

"You can have any kind of wedding you want." My father used to say with numbing regularity when we had his favorite melon for dessert. "You can have a Muslim wedding. You can have a Buddhist wedding. You can even (and this, him being a Jew, was a stretch) have a Catholic wedding," he would say. "But you can't elope!" With that he'd dig his spoon into the orange-fleshed melon of his punchline and chuckle to himself. I would groan, and my mother would usually laugh softly in a supportive manner. He loved his jokes so much, and so many of them were so bad.

I was still single when he died, but my unmarried status never seemed to frustrate my parents as it did me. I never felt the pressure to get married or to start a family that other women report. I never felt scorn from them, or the anxiety that I was somehow adrift without a mate. Except for those times when he got as wound up in my heartbreaks as I did, I thought of my father as basically content with life. I told myself he was happily married and happy to stay out of my affairs. But after he died, I realized that I really had no clue about his feelings on marriage or about my seemingly endless string of brief relationships. I realized that I had assumed too much, and that I knew very little about my parents' marriage, or about my father as a husband.

My mother rarely talked about my father for the first few years after he passed away, at least not to me. She did not say his name or refer to him. His jokes did not get repeated, and his jovial bon-homie seemed forgotten. For the first few years after his death it was as if he had never existed, except that the vortex of pain around any mention of him made its pull felt in too many conversations.

I suspected one reason why, back in those silent times, my mother chose not to go too near that tugging grief. I knew that his sick years, particularly the final one, had drained her, replaced a load of good memories with bitter ones. And that his half-hearted try at suicide when the pain from the cancer grew too much to bear left her feeling guilty and outgunned. "We'll always have Paris," he had joked, weakly, when he came to in the emergency room. But that was as good as it was going to get again. As his lucid hours shrank to minutes, I think she felt relieved, as well, as the constant waiting drew to a close. And I suspect her guilt over this relief mounted in his final days, magnified by her decision to call an ambulance for him and exacerbated as his soft fondness grew distant, confused, and then angry.

And so his memory lay like a great, sinking presence between us whenever I went over to her house for dinner. We had developed an irregular custom of having dinner together on Sunday evenings after my parents had retired to a condo near me. And as she and I carefully, gingerly, resumed this custom after his death, I wondered what kind of marriage my parents had had. Before his death, I had only seen the side of him that was devoted to her—devoted to us all, really, although his love could take the kind of clumsy action that made itself more dear by intent. But as I questioned my own relationship with him and my ties to the men who had come and gone in my life, I was beginning to see the shadows behind the bad jokes and silly stories, the bruises inflicted by his brand of lumbering love.

Since he'd died, for example, I had never seen my mother wearing the big gold and diamond earrings he'd given her for their twenty-fifth anniversary. Even I, then a child, could have warned him off their ungraceful anchor-shaped design, their awkward and heavy cut. Was she disappointed when she opened the box, hoping for something beautiful and sparkling that would reflect the years she had stood faithfully by him? Did she feel guilty for not loving such a pricey gift? She never let me know. She wore them for every big occasion, loyally donning them for doctors' dances and nights at the opera. But after his death, they never again pulled down her ears. Sentiment, memories of love lost, can be painful, I thought at first.

Early on, I had my own experiences of his misguided generosity, a spirit that I told myself was large and kind but perhaps did not accurately perceive the objects of its desire. There was, for example, the Partridge Family record he gave me for my eleventh birthday. I'd wanted it since it came out, but I had been saving up for months and had, in fact, already bought it. My mother must have been with me at its purchase—how else would I have gotten to the Modell's record counter, a car-ride away? But she had not been consulted, and when he presented it to me she kept quiet as I thanked him and feigned glee. Nor did she say anything when I smuggled my own copy out of my room, later, and hid it in the attic, for fear that he would see the duplication when he came up to kiss me goodnight. He meant well, I told myself, and he tried so hard, which I venture she also told herself as she opened her jewelry box, as she fingered the catch on those heavy bejeweled anchors. How fragile was this man, that we found ourselves protecting him? Or were there other factors at work?

She hadn't always colluded to keep him happy. She hadn't always censored herself. I remember coming home from what must have been my first year away at summer camp. My parents took me straight from the camp bus to my favorite pizza parlor. I was telling them stories about my adventures, I recall, and he was looking through the sugar packets stacked in their metal holder. I paused, and he pulled out one with a picture of a bird to show me. "It's a blue bird, just for you," he said, handing me the packet. "Oh, she's a big girl now," I remember my mom said, gently pushing his hand away, and I remember the disappointment on his face as he restacked the pretty packet. She thought, I am sure, that she was saving my newfound dignity. That I did not want to be bothered by such babyish things at the grand age of eight. Maybe I would have been embarrassed by him, had she not intervened. But what I remember now is that my father was reaching out to me, sweetly and on what he believed were my terms. I was angry at her for correcting him, and even then wanted to comfort him for trying.

Before my father died, I had always believed my parents had a good marriage. I had seen how devoted my father was to my mother: the flowers he would bring her on birthdays, holidays, and anniversaries; the obvious pride he took in the way she looked all done up for their big nights out. I wanted someone to look at me that way, to treat me that way. It seemed strange to me that until my father died I was unable to find that kind of mate, to cement that kind of a caring, loving relationship.

It wasn't as if I spent much of my twenties and early thirties alone. And whenever I became involved with a man my commitment was—at least for the duration—total. "Can't you wait awhile?" I remember one friend complaining, exasperated, when some new beau beckoned. "You're going to start seeing him, and then we'll never get to hang out anymore."

I thought she was being silly. Didn't most of our circle tend toward serial monogamy, bringing first one man and then another to our parties and to see the bands we all followed in Boston's lively circuit of clubs? Besides, as she could have pointed out, most of the time I got too caught up in a man he proved to be bad for me. Smart and mean was my usual downfall. Often these men were critics from the publications where I worked. I told myself that I liked them because they were journalists like myself. But I deliberately overlooked the fact that they made their living pinpointing the flaws and weaknesses in others' works, and eventually, in their cool, dispassionate ways, in me as well, dissecting my taste, my figure, my friends, and my lifestyle as clinically and heartlessly as if it were some stranger's packaged offering. When I was at my most honest, I could admit that this same discrimination, this sometime snobbishness, was part of their appeal. I felt honored when they chose me, and thus had to accept their judgment when they finally rejected me. And reject me they did, for as many reasons as there were men.

There was O., who hounded me to lose weight and—with equal vehemence—to write in a more stripped-down style, as if I could be tougher and leaner and still be myself. There was M., for whom I was overly emotional, and C., to whom I was not sensitive enough, or so he said. As one girlfriend pointed out, back when I was too disconsolate to listen, I sought out the type of guys who claimed to know me better than I knew myself. The kind who wanted to make me "better," or remake me in the image of their ideal. The problem was, she could have added, they weren't always generous with how they used this information.

Not all of my boyfriends were like that, although even I recognized the pattern as I drifted from my twenties to my thirties and saw my friends form more permanent alliances. Sometimes I ran across a true sweetheart, but these relationships never seemed to last either. From these, however, I could have learned something about my own weaknesses. I remember one man in particular, whom I started seeing a few months after one of my sharp cads had dumped me publicly, in the middle of a cocktail party. Rob was the opposite of the cool, cruel type. He was romantic and affectionate. And if he wasn't exactly career track, with his low-fi band, his slacker friends, and his hourly wage job, at least he was generous with what he had. He gave me flowers, more often carnations than roses, and he never stinted on hugs and approval, all of which went far toward making me feel like a whole human being again.

We'd been seeing each other for a few months when I finally decided to introduce him to my parents. Yes, I was nervous about their reaction, but I reassured myself that all would be well. My parents were open minded. They were modern. And if Rob didn't mind that I had the better paying job, the newer car, why should they? After hearing my sob stories, and seeing me retreat to the family home for long, weepy weekends after one breakup or another, they should be glad that I was seeing a man who truly cared for me. Rob, I had told them often enough, made me happy.

The evening, as I recall, started off well. Rob was very willing to meet my folks. He was ready to talk about chess with my father and music with my mother. He offered to help in the kitchen in the open, friendly way that to me had always indicated a lack of pretense and a real interest in the lives of others.

That interest was not reciprocated. Although I cannot remember at what point in the evening I first noticed it, I clearly remember the bands of tension tightening around my chest. I saw my father closing down. He did not need to say anything. I could tell by the way his mouth set too tightly, his lips slightly pursed, that he had made up his mind. All the emotional support Rob had given to me didn't count for much. I felt my breath going shallow, my face growing flushed. And when I looked back at Rob, I too saw the worn spots in his jeans and the way his long hair hung, somewhat disarrayed, over his collar. I no longer noticed how warm he was, how willing to engage them on their turf. I heard what was missing in his conversation, how the joking references he and I shared sounded silly and childish, and I almost hated him for not being more restrained, more formal. More like my father. I don't think I ever looked at him with quite the same affection again.

If we are being honest with ourselves, most of us will usually admit to some connection between the men we choose to love (if indeed men are the objects of our desire) and the first man who loves us. He may look like our father, or he may possess other traits that we attributed to him, and for many of us the similarity is irresistible. "The first man I was really attracted to was just like my father—tall, dark, handsome, aloof—and with that same ability to see my soul," one woman tells me. "I hung onto him like a rodeo rider." Conversely, we may react against our dads, seeking men who seem utterly different. "Any man who was remotely like my father would repulse me utterly," another woman explains. Either way, our dads hover over our relationships.

How could they not? According to every theorist, back to Freud, our fathers are the first love of the opposite sex, the basis of every romantic relationship we have in later life. These partners may be very different from our fathers, but our emotions toward them may be more about our fathers than about the mates we tell ourselves we have freely chosen. And what we believe are the free impressions of our heart may in fact be shadows, impressing upon us with their darkness the shape of the object that has obscured the sun.

Triggering a Need

There are many factors that play into why we settle down when we do, and with whom. Sometimes we hit a certain age, a landmark birthday, and feel compelled to cross a similar relationship threshold. Sometimes we've achieved a level of success (or disillusionment) with our professional and creative lives, and seek to focus our energies elsewhere. Maybe, we've simply dated enough, and been alone long enough, that we finally know what kind of relationship we want and we know ourselves and the people we love well enough to find ways of working out the details. Perhaps it is as simple as finally meeting someone we can love. All these factors certainly can come into play. Often more than one does, and not infrequently such factors seem to fall into place as we lose our fathers. Although several elements may be at work, the anecdotal evidence is overwhelming. Many women who have wanted to settle down, who have been through strings of unsatisfactory relationships or short-lived, unsatisfying marriages, seem to finally be able to form commitments when they lose their fathers.

It may be a basic equation of "lose one, gain one" keeping our hearts in some kind of equilibrium. "When there is a loss of a very valuable bond, people are more likely to seek a replacement," explains psychologist Froma Walsh. "We have a heightened need to make that commitment, or to seek someone who is going to fill the emotional needs that were filled by the father."

Perhaps the death makes the passage of time more real, signaling to us—as that thirtieth, thirty-fifth, or fortieth birthday otherwise might—that the time is right for us to settle down. The idea that a death, particularly the death of a parent, is a turning point in our own lives makes intuitive sense. "It's coming to terms," explains Terry Hargrave, Texas-based marriage and family therapist and editor of *The Aging Family*. "You can't have a parent die and not realize that you're next in line. That existentially moves you somewhere else. You realize that life is limited." For many people, Hargrave says, such a loss is a signal to focus on what is lasting. For most of us, love and attachments suddenly become more important. "We come to the conclusion that what we leave in terms of relationships is what is going to last."

Losing a mother, by comparison, seems to have less impact on our love lives, say the psychologists and sociologists who study the ways in which we learn and develop. Instead, it is the loss of the opposite-gender parent that for both men and women can trigger a desire for commitment to a replacement relationship. For women in particular, says Walsh, "the father is kind of a model for a mate, for better or worse."

While this urgency, this sense of timeliness and desire to connect, is not peculiar to women, factors do exist that make it more important to us. Despite the broadening of our options and the slow leveling of some gender differences, we still tend to focus on interpersonal connections as much as on other sources of status and satisfaction, at least more than our brothers and sons do. Women, for various societal reasons, tend to be more involved in the maintenance of relationships. We still seem to be "kinship keepers" much much more than men. Therefore, when we desire compensation, we look for a relationship. Our balances are kept in our hearts.

These theories explain our desire, but they do not pinpoint why so many of us suddenly are able to achieve such a connection. Many of us have held relationships at a high value before our fathers' death and still have not been able to attain or maintain them. And many of us who have since found some kind of lasting love describe our earlier dating histories as frustrating and limited. As I hear others' stories of wanting love, of valuing romance and intimacy but not being able to find it, I remember all the years that I wanted closeness in vain, throwing myself into pairings that didn't—that *couldn't*—last. I remember all the time spent trying to make myself into the woman that my man of the moment seemed to desire—losing weight and gaining it, dressing up and dressing down, and generally acting in ways that were foreign to me. I remember one wiser friend advising, with a touch of bitterness over her own experiences, "Yeah, and if I could dance on the bar and pick up the quarters without using my hands, maybe then he'd really love me." All in the desperate effort to achieve closeness.

But like so many of us, I wouldn't be able to find it until I lost my father. Then, suddenly, it became easy. Why, then, could I—could so many of us—now achieve intimacy?

Most theorists tend to attribute our newfound romantic success to two disparate reactions, both specifically linked to fathers. For them, the question does not focus on found happiness, but on our prior inability to find romantic fulfillment. For them our ability to find love is the norm, how we should be, and they link our years of loneliness to either the uncomfortable closeness we felt with our fathers or a damaging amount of distance that had existed.

The first theory postulates that many of us may remain single while our fathers are alive because we do not have room for other men in our lives. On one level, they point out, this can be a healthy reaction. With a strong, involved father, we have not felt the desperate longing that others experience. We do not, in short, have as pressing a need for a mate, *any* mate. "If your father's been a main support system, you are not so dependent on another relationship to give you those same things," explains Hargrave.

Even in such best-case scenarios, where the father-daughter relationship is healthy and mature, its loss may trigger our need for another relationship. Our loss leaves us feeling vulnerable, explains Thelma Jean Goodrich, director of behavioral science in the family residency training program at the University of Texas-Houston Medical School. "In our minds, no matter what age we are, still in our culture our father represents a shield," she says. "To lose a father makes you feel exposed, in a dangerous way."

No wonder, then that the loss of a father often evokes in us a desire for male company, for what Valerie, whose father died nearly a decade ago, calls "a longing for male energy." We may feel more vulnerable, more in need of a mate. If our relationship with our fathers was less than ideal—that is, if our need also feeds off our guilt or other vulnerabilities remaining from our connection with our father—we may pay a very high price for the new pairing, and for its illusion of temporary security.

Raquel, for example, had been single all through her father's three-year battle with bone cancer. But the week she returned from his funeral, she began an intense relationship with a man that quickly escalated from being verbally to physically abusive. Although she'd worked hard to develop an independent life, her studio apartment became more of a battleground than a home, the scene of fights and broken furniture. In a way, she wasn't surprised by her vulnerability to such a violent relationship: her parents' marriage had been rocky at best, and her father had been known to slap his wife and daughter, and to whip his one son with a belt. But Raquel had managed to avoid that pattern in her own life—until her father was no longer there. "I was definitely looking for Daddy," she says now. The result was what she now recalls as "the worst relationship of my life."

What she finds hard to understand in retrospect is not how she got into the relationship, but that she was clearly ambivalent about ending it. "I was cheating on him right and left," she recalls. "I stopped coming home." Several times she broke it off, but each time he would apologize, and she would take him back. After nearly a year of such violent back and forth, she moved to another city, largely to escape her boyfriend's rages. But when he called her, as he always did, lonely and sorrowful, she invited him to come stay with her and look for work in her new hometown. The honeymoon did not last, and the smacks and the pushes began getting worse. Finally, nearly two years after her father's death, she found her footing again and ended the relationship for good.

"I got tired of being thrown up against walls. I got tired of his temper, and I got tired of *him*. At one point, I hadn't been home all night, and I walked in the next morning, and I said this is not working." Although Raquel is still sorting out the legacy of fear and violence that she inherited from her parents' marriage, she has never repeated this pattern. She has never been so vulnerable again.

Not that we necessarily need such a history to become vulnerable. Tara, for example, did not come from an abusive household.

She views herself as a fairly stable woman, one who "never needed to be on the arm of some man," as she put it. Until her father died.

The first sign that she noticed was a mild but surprising flirtatiousness that had not previously been part of her character. "I was flirting with the computer salesman on the phone. I had a crush on the priest," she says now. "Stuff I never really did before."

While this passage was harmless, what was to come was not. Two months after her father's funeral, she hooked up with an old acquaintance, a man she knew well but had always steered clear of, in part because she knew his general misogyny had caused his two marriages to fail. Soon, they were constant companions, and she found that he was putting her life at risk.

"I had a hard time accepting what had happened," she says now. In retrospect, the escalating danger was clear. First, he exposed her to sexually transmitted diseases without apology or explanation. Then, he took her rock climbing without proper safety equipment. When she called him on his unsafe behavior, he threatened to break up with her and she apologized. Finally, three months later, while they were climbing again, he left her stranded on top of a hundred-foot cliff as night fell. She was able to descend on her own, but was sufficiently shaken to end the relationship. What puzzles her now is why she got into it in the first place.

"People had said to me, 'You shouldn't get involved with somebody so soon after your father's death.' All of that came back to me at that point and I thought there has got to be something here. He gave me every indication of what a misogynist he was, but I didn't want to accept it."

Breaking the Chain

These women did what many of us do, responding to the loss of a father by "filling in the blank" with another man, often making unwise moves and taking up with dangerous companions in the wake of our loss. For others among us, however, this loss triggers the opposite reaction, allowing us to finally end years of addictive relationships with inappropriate partners. Freed by the absence of the imposing male presence of our fathers, we may finally be able to express our real needs and find mates or lifestyles that will fulfill us. We, too, react to loss, but we are, perhaps, the ones whose "good daddies" were a little too present in our lives. And while this sounds incestuous, implying that we have never resolved that first Freudian attraction to our fathers, the truth is more complicated, more subtle, and sometimes more treacherous. We loved our dear daddies and wanted to please them, which usually meant acting in certain ways: achieving good grades or making ourselves fit a certain style. And as we grew up, because of this pressure, this highly rewarded ability to please and to perform, we often found ourselves unbalanced in our adult relationships. Continuing as we did when we were little, we never learned how to balance the traditional feminine role of defining ourselves by our importance to others with a healthy focus on our own desires.

Cara, for example, traveled across the globe, emigrating from Germany to the United States to establish herself professionally. She loved her parents, and felt particularly close to her father, with whom she shared a lively, inquisitive intelligence and a wide-eyed appreciation of the world. Unfortunately, she realizes now, several years after his death, her hunger for his approval was matched by his thirst for her brilliance, her companionship, and support.

"There was a sense that my dad needed me," she says. Talking about her youth, she invariably comes around to the concerts to which he took her rather than her mother. She recalls the books he shared with her and the way he would seek her, rather than her mother, to discuss politics, history, and art. The interests and the attention fed each other, and she grew closer to him. "Ultimately I think I felt more attached to my dad than my mother. I was needed more in various ways by him than by her."

Although she had made a brief, early marriage, she explains, nobody in her family was much surprised when that union fell apart. And for the decade that followed, she found her relation-

ships all tended to be rather shallow and unfulfilling. "I was
involved with someone when my dad died," she looks back. "He
was somebody who couldn't commit to me and I made a big fuss
out of it. In hindsight, maybe I couldn't commit to him either. But
I couldn't break up with him till my dad was dead." Soon after
returning from his funeral, she was able to end that relationship.
Within the year she was seeing the man who is now her husband:
"I couldn't say that all of a sudden this relationship magically
didn't have any issues," she says. What was different was the way
she approached the relationship. Suddenly, she says, "it was possible to make a commitment, and to make a commitment to working things out."

With her father, Cara had fulfilled the traditional role of pla-
cater, of pleasing companion. On her own, finally, she was able
to find a balance between her needs and her willingness to
accommodate her partner. "My father's death definitely set me
free to get involved with someone and make a clear commitment," she says.

Of course, sometimes our fathers were too much in our lives in
more clearly negative ways. Although we may not have realized
this consciously, we often acted on it, fleeing from commitment
while they were alive. When our connections to our fathers were
argumentative and unhappy, any alliance with a man might have
felt like capitulation. "Did I want to get married? Of course I did!"
Irina laughs at the idea that she spent her first forty years avoiding
marriage. She admits, however, that her rebellion against her
father may have intruded on her earlier attempts to settle down. "I
never wanted anybody to tell me what to do," she recalls. "I
broke up with this one guy because he said, 'One day, when
you're older . . .' which my father used to say. I ended the relationship right there." Any man who in any way evoked her father
could cause her to flee.

Now that her father is gone, however, Irina finds that she has
learned to accept his better traits. Before his death, she says, she
was not particularly interested in Chuck, one of several men she

was dating. Somehow, she just didn't feel the click. She told herself that this was because he was too ardently pursuing her, that he was too old and had been married before, which she disliked. But after her father died, her excuses lost their potency. They have been happily married now for seven years. "I see so many ways that they're alike," she can say now. "The way he can happily expound on a subject; he's very social. And he's very handsome. My father was always incredibly well dressed, and Chuck's the same way. I look at Chuck coming through the door, and I think of my father," she says. Now that her father is gone, this similarity is no longer a problem.

Such a reaction had kept Lita from the kind of happy domesticity she craved, as well. Now thirty-seven, Lita is planning her marriage to Mark for this spring. They've already bought a house together and with him she has found the kind of contentment that two years ago, when her father was alive, she was not sure was possible. She doubted she could even have such domestic happiness, in part, she acknowledges, because of her virulently negative feelings toward her emotionally abusive father, a paranoid and cynical man who had frequently accused Lita and her mother of plotting against him and of gloating in his disappointments. After leaving the family home that he had darkened with his gloom, she strove to avoid any man who bore the slightest resemblance to her father. The result, she now believes, was that she had also pushed away any man who displayed his few good traits, such as his serious and studious side and his deep, if often unstated, caring.

"Since I've been with Mark, I've begun to notice attractive things about him that remind me of the best things about my father. And whether I could have stomached them, been able to separate my father's good qualities from his bad qualities, is unclear." Lita, a former professor of law, has inherited her father's intellectual rigor. But her romantic history had not involved many men who were as smart or as strong as she is.

"Whether I would have avoided someone with *any* of his qualities while he was alive is unclear. There's something about sitting next to Mark in synagogue and hearing him recite Hebrew that reminds me of my father," she notes. "If my father were still alive, I might have found that repulsive."

For women who define themselves as bisexual or lesbian, the loss of a father may take on added significance, particularly if our fathers were not aware of this part of our lives. Sexuality, which is a tense subject for any woman to discuss with her father, too often became the big secret, the key to ourselves that did not get shared. Denise, for example, was working up the courage to come out to her parents when her father died suddenly of heart attack. They had been close, although she had resisted telling him about her sexual orientation, in part because she was not yet comfortable with this part of herself. But living away from home for the first time, she had come to terms with who she was, and she wanted to be open. "His dying robbed me of that," she says with regret. Although she wants to believe that he loved her, she continues, she'll never be sure. "I like to think that he would have accepted me and loved me for who I am, but I will never know."

Although this secret may be only one of many issues that we have to resolve alone, after our fathers' death, it is so central to who we are and how we live that it can leave us vulnerable and unsure. Even fathers we knew loved us may have been unintentionally and subtly inhibiting—and hurtful. Nella, who is now in a happy and stable relationship with a woman, also never really knew how her father would respond to her sexuality. But because she had overheard him making homophobic jokes in her presence, she felt she could never take the risk of finding out. Her fear of rejection was so acute that she delayed coming out—to herself as well as to her parents—during his lifetime. "With my father it was something that I didn't want to approach," she recalls. "It would have been too painful."

Although she describes her relationship with both her parents as generally loving and warm, she reacted to her father's careless verbal abuse by shutting herself off from the relationships that would have fulfilled her. Instead, she dated men, including some nice guys whom she grew quite fond of, and denied the attraction she long felt for women. "It never occurred to me that women were datable," she says now.

The pattern of denial became most pronounced after her father died and she responded by getting seriously involved with a friend's male cousin. Only after a few months, she says, could she see how she was overreacting and how wrong that relationship was. Behind this ill-fated straight romance, she finally understood her own fear of rejection and guilt about not being the daughter she imagined her father had wanted. In retrospect, she realizes that this relationship was her last stab at reshaping herself in her father's image of who she should be.

"If there was a chance that I was straight, then whatever had stood between me and my dad wasn't a lie," she explains her reasoning in retrospect. "But that relationship never jelled. It never made sense as anything other than a friendship." As her mourning eased, she realized the futility of her unconscious charade, particularly when she was "whacked between the eyes" by a new crush on a female classmate. Her father's looming presence—with all the prejudices he may or may not have held—passed, and she was finally able to seek out secure and loving relationships with women.

The Wrong Man

Not every woman who cannot connect will find the source of her problem in a father who was too present, who was somehow too powerful or uncomfortably close. Strangely, the same earlier inability to form lasting, loving relationships may have its roots in the opposite kind of father-daughter interaction or in a confused combination of the two, which is all the more difficult to decipher. Although in many ways our former long-lasting loneliness (and our new ability to find and to keep love) may appear the same as the reaction to a too-close father, it may also have sprung from too much distance. Instead of a father who loomed large in our lives for good or ill, we may have had one who was uninvolved, or seemed to be uncaring. Just as too-present fathers may have made us unconsciously resist or mistrust closeness, absent fathers may have overly occupied our hearts, hindering us from completing any other connection. Simply put, if we didn't get the kind of love or support we wanted from our fathers, we might have remained single during their lifetimes because these needs were unresolved at their most basic daughter-father level. We were still waiting for Daddy. And this unfulfilled desire kept us on hold, unable to move forward, and even in the self-destructive patterns so many of us recognize.

Women in unsatisfying or even masochistic relationships, theorists such as Jessica Benjamin explain, may not really understand how to fall in love in a healthy way. Instead of seeking partners who will love us as we are, we seek those who are what we were forbidden to be. That is, instead of finding lovers who make us feel good about ourselves, we fall for the outlaws and troublemakers, or the dependent types who always find people to care for them—out of a kind of jealousy. We lack autonomy, and so we envy their freedom to be "bad." If we are caught in this trap, as I know I was, we may be incapable of judging whether or not this type is capable of being warm, nurturing, and supportive.

For example, we may have felt a desire for independence and adventure, but our father—the person we looked to for validation of this desire—was not aware of our wishes or refused to accept or acknowledge them. Instead, he became an overprotective dad who kept us home. And the frustration we felt at being so tied down became subverted into a yearning for footloose or irresponsible men. Who we wanted to be and who we wanted to love got confused.

We all know this type of behavior. If we haven't done it, our friends have. We talk knowingly among ourselves of our habits, or our friends' habits, or walking into a cocktail party full of suitable, single professionals and zooming in on the one unemployed drug addict, temper-tossed womanizer, or con man. If he's married, so much the better.

In a most superficial way, this type of lover does give us what we want: Because a fancy-free partner does not tie us down, we end up with our independence. But although we may get a vicarious thrill out of being with these wild types, we are not feeding any of our real hungers. Because we are choosing partners for the wrong reasons, we don't usually find a satisfying love with them. We enter into these relationships with a sense that we are lacking something, and they confirm our inadequacies. They do so in a manner that is all the more captivating because it always seems, at least at first, as if they are finally giving us a chance to lose the weight, to make ourselves over, to finally get it right. But of course, we can't. Plus, although we are not tied down by them, we still feel bound by our compulsion, inhibited by our loneliness, with the result that although we are left alone, we do not feel free. The damage accumulates. Because we are unclear about our motives, we cannot understand why we are disappointed, why our sense of ourselves gets stripped down further after each encounter. This is not the kind of independence for which we bargained.

Continuing Illusions

We may never get permission from our fathers that it is okay to lead our lives. In the real world, they may never tell us that it is fine to be somewhat adventurous, or even to trade in our "good little girl" personas for a more mature image of ourselves. The strongest of us, of course, resolve these issues while our fathers are still around. But it's hard to go against such a primal attachment. And for many of us who have been waiting, that release only comes when our dads are no longer able to tut-tut our choices or glower at us over the dinner table. Then we are free, finally, to go out and be who we want. And then we are also free to get what we want, what we have wanted all along.

Rona, for example, talks of her father's clinging devotion, a caretaking quality that she found irksome. She knows he loved her. She also admits that he was worried about her, as she passed into her late thirties single, often unable to hold a steady job. Her history of tumultuous attachments made him fear that his youngest child, his baby, would never settle down. When he became ill, she was not seeing anyone, but her recent past had included romances with a difficult co-worker and a musician in a constantly touring band—neither good long-term choices for her. Once her father succumbed to his long illness and was no longer around to worry, she was finally able to accept mature care and nurturing from another man.

"I'm looking for nice now," she says. "Dangerous is out. Boys are out; men are in." In the past year, the second since her father passed away, she has developed a strong and steady relationship with a secure man. He cares about her, their mutual devotion is obvious, and for the first time, she can accept this level of attachment. "My father always was somehow encroaching on my personal emotional space by being so demanding—or what I felt was demanding. I realize now that made me somewhat emotionally unavailable. I was unwilling to be available, so I'd unconsciously go for guys who were also emotionally unavailable. Now I'm ready to accept someone being nice without seeing that as a demand." At the age of forty-three, she is finally truly free.

The Family Triangle

Sometimes we have spent years paying off an older debt. Our fathers, we must remember, were not only our parents, they were the husbands (or ex-husbands or lovers) of our mothers. Many of our deepest feelings were formed in reaction to what we witnessed in these relationships, often in our own homes. We may have learned distrust. We may have seen unhappiness or inequality, even if the tears and burdens did not fall directly on us. We may be responding not only to how our fathers treated us, but to how we saw them act toward our mothers. In many ways, we may be continuing a dance that our parents started. If we are lucky and strong and smart, once that dance has ended we may be able to recognize that we are following someone else's patterns and learn to choose our own steps.

For too long, clearly, many of us who remained single did so because we tended to re-create the inequalities we had lived with in our homes. "I was frustrated with that relationship, but I couldn't bring myself to leave it," one woman tells me. "In some way, it felt familiar." Many of us could say the same.

Cara's first marriage duplicated her parents' rather old-fashioned and unequal one. Although she can now prize her mother's pragmatic approach, all through her youth Cara saw her practical and earthy mother's judgment continuously dismissed by her intellectual father. And strangely, although Cara is a tenured professor, in her own disastrous marriage she found herself duplicating her mother's less intelligent, more emotional role, a reenactment that prompted Cara to enter psychoanalysis. "I saw myself as an equal person, but in that relationship I ended up looking like my mother," she says. "I was the one who was losing arguments." She becomes heated as she recalls the fights she and her first husband would have. "He would argue on the basis of principle, and I was arguing on the basis of emotion. And as a result, I was always coming across as less logical. After awhile I really felt like the inferior one in that relationship. I felt really bad about myself."

The question that remains for Cara is not why she divorced her first husband, but how she got into that relationship in the first place. The answer, I think, is that sometimes our offering to our fathers is not a presence, not something we do or give, but an absence, a willingness to overlook character flaws. We love our fathers and want to forgive them their human frailties, and we do so in a child's way, by pretending these failings do not exist. Unwilling to note how her adored father scorned her mother, wanting somehow for her parents' marriage to be more loving and equal than it was, she threw herself into one just like it, hoping to prove that this inequality was all right, was somehow more fine and affectionate than she had sensed as a child. Like so many of us, she duplicated the worst parts of her parents' relationship in the hope that she could magically make the marriage a good one, make the happy ending come about. As she found after years of analysis, we can't fix our parents' marriages, and often we sacrifice decades to continue the illusion, the family myth. We choose to be blind, to be single or, if married, lonely, rather than acknowledge a flaw in our parents' bond, or in our fathers.

I know how long I spent not seeing my father's worst characteristic, the gap between his temper and his generosity, between his deep love and his inability or unwillingness to see me or my mother as we actually were. I know that when I, too, gave a cold shoulder to my loving Rob I was playing along with my father. I was pretending that his snap judgment, his sudden switch from warm to cold, was wiser and more just than what I had learned through my own months of loving experience. I was choosing to believe in him rather than the man I loved. I was trusting my father rather than the evidence of my own senses.

Sometimes, when I was with men who shared my father's temper, I would simply refuse to acknowledge any problem at all. As my friend had noted, I almost always immediately immersed myself in these relationships, to the exclusion of even my oldest friends. What my friend did not understand was the reasoning that governed my head-first dives into the deep end. What I was unconsciously telling myself, I now believe, was that if I could throw myself into a relationship, if I could make it seem serious at least to myself, then there could be no reason to be afraid. Looked at another way, if I gave myself over completely to a mercurial man, then his vagaries, his sudden mood swings, must not be that bad. Almost, I convinced myself, they would not exist. And so I sought out men who carried on the worst traits of my father, men who had short tempers and were quick to judgment. Men who left me feeling not only rejected but stupid as well. But when I was with them, for as long as I could, I would tell myself that their quick rage was only the flip side of their intelligence. When they cut me apart with cool, cruel observations, I would try to believe that I could reconcile their sharp words to the playful wit that I loved, as if by the sheer force of my belief I could turn their hurtful traits into endearing ones and could find emotional fulfillment in them. I was making believe I was happy. In some way, this helped me deny the unhappiness that must have existed in my parents' marriage, to deny the flaws in my father's treatment of his wife and of me, his daughter.

I was trying to perform magic as a child would. Not very smart for a woman in her twenties and early thirties, but perhaps something that others can recognize. As Thelma Jean Goodrich, the Texas-based psychologist, puts it: "Just because you're an adult doesn't mean you have an adult relationship with your father." True enough, like a little girl, I was pretending—aggressively, wholeheartedly pretending—not to see what I didn't want to be true. Yes, my father was a dear man, and loving. But he was also capable of great cruelty. It was as if he had a bifurcated personality, as if the kind side and the cold side never met in any middle ground. And having experienced the former I knew I couldn't bear the latter. And so I spent much of my adult life pretending that these unreconciled sides, this split, never existed. I was intentionally straddling fault lines between temper and nurturance, between the two sides of my father that seemed disconnected and between parents who could not always communicate.

When my father died, I found that I could drop my magic balancing act. After his death I found I was able to see all the other men I knew more clearly and to judge our attachments more accurately. Sure, some of these connections remained pretty shallow, especially in the first few months after his death, when I was just beginning to date again, to get out of the house. But these kinds of relationships served their purpose as well, and when they were done, I found for perhaps the first time in my adult life that I could leave them without pain. A fortune teller I went to on a whim that spring confirmed my suspicions. "You like to dance," she said, laying out my cards. "The man you are with now, he is, well, he is good for dancing." She looked up from the tarot deck and straight into my face, and I laughed. She started chuckling, too, when she saw that I understood her. She was right, but I already knew what she was trying to tell me. And then, when I met Jon, the man who is now my husband, some months later, I was ready.

Would I have gone for him years before? Perhaps. We had, in fact, moved in the same social circle for about six years before we finally hooked up. And if I didn't notice his quiet intelligence, his gentle humor at first, the warmth and good sense he brought to all our interactions had certainly grown on me by the time we ran into each other at the July reunion of a band we both had loved years earlier.

"I'm sorry about your father," was the first thing he said to me. We hadn't seen each other in almost a year, I figured out later, and my father had died nearly six months before. But he was always a careful and caring man and I was warmed by his greeting. When he reached forward to give me a hug as if my loss was still fresh, I felt the kindness in him, and for once that was the most important trait of all. We chatted off and on throughout that night. At one point we both lost the friends we had come with and found ourselves dancing together, laughing over a lyric that had seemed a life-or-death matter when we were in our twenties, and by the end of that evening something in me clicked. By the end of that summer we were a couple, and we've built our lives around each other since. There's magic between us, I know that, but I also know that the timing was right. I was at a point where I could appreciate his serious approach to work and writing and not want to rail against a discipline that reminded me of my father's. I could giggle along with his silly side as well, and not worry about whether anyone else would find us both juvenile. Plus, as hard as I fell for Jon, once we started dating I was still able to talk to him—to communicate who I was and what I wanted from life and from a loving partnership, and also to accept and explain the differences between us, when they arose.

It's strange what we go through, how much of ourselves we are willing to sacrifice on the altar of domestic bliss. But it does help to explain some of the changes we experience, and how through our loss we may be freed. I thought I was a smart woman, an independent woman, and an adult. But not until my father was gone could I, like Cara, allow myself to look honestly at the men I was dating. Not until he no longer asked for my protection, my silent collaboration, could I seek out, like Rona, a partner who would be able to give me the attention and care I needed and deserved. Not until his death was I able, like Lita, to finally see the good as separate from the painful, angry, and mean parts of my father, and be able to celebrate the warmth and commitment that he had embodied in a marriage of my own. It would be simple to say that once my father was gone I had room in my life for another man, but the change was both more basic and profound. I believe at any stage in my life I would have wanted Jon. But with my father gone, there was room for me to be my own woman, and that made it possible for me to love.

CHAPTER 6

Marriages in Transition

For those of us who are married or otherwise permanently partnered when we lose our fathers, this loss can alter the roles of our spouses and partners in our lives. As these roles change, so do our feelings of adulthood and responsibility, causing many women to use the period after their fathers' deaths as a time to reevaluate long-term relationships, as well as the motivations and desires that originally led us to build these new families.

A grieving woman is a prickly person, no matter how much we wish it weren't so. Forget the pining, tear-stained heroine, that convention of sentimental novels and weepy films. The reality, for most of us who have undergone a loss, is much less palatable, and for those who love us, much harder to comfort.

After a loss we may exhibit our grief in a variety of ways. We may be tired and whiny, or aggressively active. We may take to bed for weeks, or never seem to sleep, surviving on nightmare-riddled catnaps that leave us hollow-eyed and skittish, more wraith than woman. Sexually and emotionally, we may be unresponsive or clinically detached, which can be scarier still to those around us. It is a rare woman who always responds to loss in a predictable, approachable manner. Much more common is one or all of the above reactions, which can serve to push others away just when we could most use a hug. We are generally difficult to be around.

No wonder, then, that so many women in marriages or other long-term partnerships report disruptions in these relationships in the year or two following the deaths of their fathers. When we factor in the other variables in these intimate relationships—the similarities a husband may have to a father in a wife's eyes, or the division of roles that mate and father served when both were alive—it may seem more natural for changes to occur than for things to stay the same.

I know this to be true because of Clint Eastwood. Clint Eastwood, in particular in the nameless role of the antihero that he created in his early spaghetti Westerns, was one of my two constant companions during the months immediately following my father's death.

I was neither married nor in a long-term partnership when my father died, but I had (and still have) a long-standing friendship that, at that time, had already survived such crises as heartbreaks, job changes, and one move to the West Coast that resulted in ridiculous phone bills throughout its three-year duration.

Our friendship was truly tried, however, during the final months of my father's illness, and especially during those last few weeks. For just when I felt I most needed my friend, he seemed to grow remote. Just when I wanted to talk, he grew visibly uncomfortable, the heat and darkness of what I was experiencing seemed to scare him more than the years of friendship and affection could overcome.

It is true there were complicating factors in our relationship during this time. The abusive boyfriend I had finally freed myself from had taken up much of my time in the preceding year, and I hadn't been around for my friend as much as either of us would have liked. During the last stage of that poisonous pairing, my boyfriend had grown increasingly jealous of the other people in my life, particularly those relationships that predated him and specifically my friendships with men. And for a time, I had caved in to his unreasonable demands, limiting my own availability to my older friends. By following this relationship up with an ill-fated fling immediately before my father's final hospitalization, I had once again made myself unavailable to my friend—letting my infatuation rule my heart, my mind, and once again, my time.

But we'd been through such patches before, with both of us taking turns leaving our steadier friendship for the thrall of romance or its disastrous aftermath. This was a different distance, and it made my heart sink further when I saw the pull above his brow as he looked at me with not only worry but also uneasiness. I heard the hesitation as he struggled to find the right thing to say. I could have told him that there were no right words, and that his presence alone was comforting. But I didn't. What I focused on instead was his unease. I saw his discomfort as a sign that I was truly drifting farther from the land of the living, joining my father in an unfathomable neverland of waiting and fear.

And then it was over. My father died, and with him the only impetus I could find for holding myself together outside of work. I functioned, overfunctioned perhaps, in the office, and I kept trying to make myself available to my mother. But at night, when I was home in my own apartment, the batteries ran down. I found myself sitting in front of the television, wanting nothing more than a narrative to occupy me until the early hours of the morning, when—at two, at three, or four in the morning—I could finally retire to bed with something like assurance that soon I would fall into the dreamless sleep of exhaustion.

I don't remember how I came upon Clint Eastwood's oeuvre.
At that time my taste ran more to quirky comedies, romances, and
the kind of movies like *Desperately Seeking Susan* that affirmed my
own life choices, or at least established the battle lines between the
bohemian and the suburban. I imagine I caught one of Eastwood's
masterpieces on television during those wakeful nights. I must
have stumbled into one of those long, silent shots of desert that
slowly focus in on stubble and squint, and recognized in the
extended, understated simmer of those eyes the kind of detach-
ment to which I aspired. However I found these movies, the effect
was immediate. I was hooked.

The spaghetti Westerns were first. These films, which were
(and have continued to be) my favorites, filled my nights, first with
the nameless gunslinger of *Fistful of Dollars* and *For a Few Dollars
More* and soon with the bitter outcast of *The Outlaw Josie Wales*, a
man so alienated he refuses to acknowledge the victory of the
hated Union army over his Missouri company. The comedies and
war movies followed, and somewhere in there, so did my friend.

I had enough sense, enough taste to be more than mildly
embarrassed by my yen for Clint. I recognized that my growing
infatuation for the eternally cool, proto-grunge outcast had down-
right appalling political implications. I knew that in my cynical
antihero there lurked the heart of a right-wing conservative, that
those shootings were meant as metaphor for an entire approach to
life. And as a feminist and a liberal I was ashamed, even if he had a
strong jaw and eyes more piercingly blue than this Jewish girl had
ever experienced up close. I also knew I couldn't hide my growing
infatuation from the staff of the local Videosmith, but I pretended
I could by avoiding eye contact with the clerks who checked out
my movies—two, sometimes three, tapes several nights each week.
One of them blew my cover, becoming perhaps unintentionally
the first person to reach me in my haze. One evening, on checking
me out, he ventured a suggestion: "Have you tried *Delta Force?* Of
the war Eastwoods, I think it's one of the best." As I recall, I
thanked him—film buff to film buff, of course—and then put the

suggestion out of my mind. For me, the appeal of Eastwood was in those Westerns—the perpetual and hopelessly romantic loner.

The attraction was obvious: even beyond the high-plains sky-blue eyes, Eastwood's character in these movies was the ideal—the strong, quiet man. My father had often been silent, too, but more often because he was perplexed rather than determined. In comparison to my father's befuddled, clumsy bear, Eastwood was a tiger, stalking. He was powerful in his silence, and (as the long shots of his piercing glance made clear) that silence hid a great depth of feeling. Sure, he might have seemed lawless, but by the film's end it would always be obvious that he obeyed a deeper moral code as he gave his hard-earned thievings to the young family or came back, just one more time, to fight for the widders and orphans. Nor was he completely invulnerable to beauty or, ultimately, to love. When he whispered "Show me" to Sondra Locke toward the end of *Josie Wales*—finally giving up the angry celibacy he'd maintained since the Union soldiers slaughtered his family—his previous rugged silence setting his few words of love (or proposition) in high relief, I could have swooned.

Not that romance softened him any. No matter how battered and bruised he was, no matter who he'd left behind, he'd manage to come back fighting one last time, shooting like fireworks. And by the story's end, he'd ride away, unbroken in spirit if not in limbs, and disappear bravely over the horizon in search of the next adventure or damsel in distress. He was unbeatable. He was never overwhelmed by plumbing or by a family. And, unlike my dad, he never died.

He never squirmed either, unlike my friend. But although my friend could not be Clint Eastwood (or my father), he did prove himself during those long winter months, sitting with me through multiple viewings of the better films and even, once, through both tapes of what must be the star's personal low point: *Paint Your Wagon*. ("Clint sings!" the box said, and the less added to that, the better.) What's more, when I began to run through all the titles available at the local Videosmith and was wasting money on repeat rentals, my friend offered to copy the movies I rented, risking copyright laws and hours of additional boredom to provide me with what I seemed to need, the filmic fodder that filled my long, wakeful nights.

In short, he was there, providing company when he couldn't offer comfort. And gradually I was able to open up, to will myself to forgive him for the obvious discomfort he had felt during the earlier part of my crisis and for his inability to soothe my pain. Together we mended a relationship that had become a little frayed, and by spring he had jollied me out of my apartment and back to the music clubs that had once been a mainstay of my social life. He made me have fun again, and ultimately brought me back into contact with Jon. Through his constancy, my friend reintroduced me to humanity and into the world of the living. And when Jon and I were married, my friend was standing beside us, supporting the *chuppah* (the canopy) that in part symbolizes the community of love and friendship we share.

As I've said, my friendship with this man wasn't a marriage, but it was, and continues to be, a reliable, long-term relationship, and in some simple ways it can serve as a model for one element of marriage, that of steady companionship. For your mate, if you have one, is likely the person you turn to for comfort. And when the pain is so great, the loss so profound that it must be endured rather than salved, it is this kind of relationship that bears the burden. At times the endless series of thankless tasks may be too much for a particular partner and the mourning too heavy for the relationship, which can be injured or even broken under the strain. Sometimes the problem isn't grief, but simply communication: when we ourselves do not understand why we are reacting as we do, our partners may be excused if they are confused by us. They may be stymied by our mood swings, frightened by our hopelessness, not recognizing these as expressions of normal grief and mourning. Sometimes those closest to us are simply incapable of dealing with death; sometimes, like my friend, they are so frightened by the reality of what we are facing that they are unable to be their usual sympathetic, nurturing selves.

"My husband really had no clue how to deal with this," says Kyra, recalling the deep grief that shook her world after her father's death last year. "He couldn't understand the hopelessness and despair I was feeling." Kyra's loss colored her view of the world in the months following her father's death, turning the future she and her husband had planned together temporarily dark. "I thought to myself that I didn't want to have kids because I never wanted them to go through what I was going through. After Dad's death, all I could see in the news and in other people's tragedies had me focusing on the temporariness of life and the fragility of it all." This deep grief drove a wedge between Kyra and her husband, despite prior years of devotion.

"It's been hard for my husband," says Kyra. "He's never gone through a similar thing; he's just not at the same place I am. He wants to understand, but he really can't. And I think it feels like I'm pushing him to be where I am."

Rocking a Marriage

Death isn't catching, I want to tell Kyra's husband and all our confused and temporarily helpless partners. But loneliness is, and if our partners withdraw into confusion and fear during this crisis, just when we need them so much, then we, already hindered by our troubles, experience a double abandonment. At times, our partners' confusion and withdrawal may feel like betrayal, and sometimes this is too much for us to easily forgive. At its worst, it may seem to reveal a fault line in the partner's character, proving him or her to be unreliable in times of crisis.

When her father died last year, after a long battle with Alzheimer's, Marcy felt emotionally deserted by her husband. Although he was physically present throughout her father's illness and final decline, he held himself apart, remaining remote and withdrawing into work just when she needed his support, both for herself and for their three children, who picked up on the anxiety and tension in the home. "I felt I was in a total vacuum," she says, looking back. "My husband wasn't there for me. He just receded. And it was hard not to show my kids how distressed I was, and so I became an emotional wreck. I ended up in the hospital myself. I thought I was having a heart attack."

Although this crisis has passed, its memory has left Marcy shaken, her faith in her husband damaged perhaps beyond repair. "I am thinking and rethinking my relationship with my husband," she says, chewing over the topic that won't go away. They have broached the subject of separating, which Marcy finds very frightening after nearly a decade of marriage. However, that fear has not obscured her trauma or her sense of abandonment. "I'm a little clearer about what I want," she says, explaining that she regards this crisis as a foreshadowing of what growing old with her husband might be like. "You get some insight into what might happen in the future," she says, "and you want someone who will be there for you." After seeing how her husband reacted during her father's illness and death, she lacks the confidence that he will be a supportive partner as they both age.

The distance or discomfort that rock a long-term relationship after such a loss may also have to do with our partners' own grief over our fathers' deaths. Particularly in cases where our partners were closer to our fathers than to their own, they may be grieving, too, and their pain must be acknowledged. To some extent, we all join with our partners' families, as well as with the individuals with whom we live. For some of us, however, our family may be almost as important as we are to our union. If our partners came into the relationship looking, at some level, to replace their own birth family with ours, then the death of our fathers may upset the basic underpinnings of our unions. For couples facing such a situation, the challenge is not only in grieving a deeply shared loss and supporting each other, but in redefining the partnership as a relationship between two adults.

Anna's father, for example, was nearly as important a player in her marriage as she or her husband Kip. Without him, their focus and their linchpin, these two adults found themselves in the roles of lost children, at loose ends with each other and foundering without his guidance.

"We always spent so much time with him," she says, recalling the man who died unexpectedly two years ago. "But since Daddy died I think we both have been trying to figure out what to do. He chose to work more," she says of her husband, who had found in his father-in-law the adoring parent his own father had not been. "We started to travel a little bit, but my husband is not a real good traveler. We try to do things that we could do together. It always seemed like we needed something more."

Although Anna won't say so openly, it's clear she feels somewhat let down by Kip, who is still burying himself in his work. In retrospect, it seems he is expressing stronger feelings about his father-in-law than about his wife.

Not that our partners are always the ones causing the rift. For what we may discover at this juncture is just how important our fathers were to our relationships. We may find that our fathers held such an exalted position in our lives, either because of our worshipful love or because of the unresolved mix of love and fear that we had for them, that we joined with partners we considered subordinate.

I have been writing, primarily, of heterosexual relationships, marriages and domestic partnerships—and certainly our fathers were men. But after speaking to dozens of women, straight and lesbian, I feel confident that many of the issues we share are the same, whether we are married to men or permanently partnered to other women. In fact, recent writings by psychologists and social workers, such as Smith College professor emerita Joan Laird, reveal that lesbians are often just as tightly connected to their families of origin—that is their parents—as straight women, for better and for worse. My own research has confirmed this. After interviewing seventy women, and talking informally with dozens more,

I believe marriages and same-sex partnerships deal with almost all the same problems and emotions. Not that we are all the same, but just as our individual pairings are always unique so too our general patterns tend to be shared by all of us. Women in both types of relationships have told me of finding their father's best—and worst—traits in their mates, and have detailed their reactions to these sometimes startling discoveries. Women in both types of committed, monogamous relationships have also talked with me candidly of the patterns they saw in their parents' interactions, roles and responsibilities that have been absorbed unconsciously and played out or rejected in dealings with mates. Therefore, I have tried to mingle the two types of relationships while writing of women and love, with a few exceptions.

For women in conventional heterosexual marriages, for example, the loss of a father may be more likely to make visible to us the subtle beliefs we have about men in general, and the parallels between our dads and our husbands. For some of us, clearly, the classic Freudian model has a different twist. Instead of separating from our fathers and marrying men who reminded us of them, we have married men we view as supplements, secondary males who are fine as long as our fathers are around to provide the real thing. This kind of bonding may have served numerous purposes. Such a mate, for example, posed no real threat to the father-daughter bond, and when we felt unable or unwilling to replace that bond, this kind of relationship gave us the appearance of independent adulthood without the price. As long as we kept the balance right, we may have been blissfully happy in such a triangular relationship. However, once father has gone the remaining union may become as unstable as a stool with only two legs. Instead of having it all, our inability to give up some closeness to our fathers now leaves us with less than a marriage, much like the situation that Anna and Kip are facing.

For Lillian, the loss of her father has revealed the lack of passion in her marriage. Her problem, as she now can describe it, came about in part because she never resolved the intense feelings of love and repulsion she felt about her father and about her parents' marriage. For Lillian, her attraction to the qualities she loved in her father had always battled with the dislike she felt at the strict gender roles played out in her parents' marriage, roles that she had believed were a necessary corollary to his strong personality. The resulting conflict influenced her choice of her husband Matt, a man she describes as relatively weak. Although he undoubtedly has strengths of which she is not aware, to Lillian, he is "less than a man." While her father was alive, he provided a masculine component in her life. Now that he is out of the picture, she is realizing how unsatisfied she is with the husband she sees as a smaller, less effective version.

"I realized after my father died that I had wanted to marry somebody like my dad and I very much wanted to marry somebody *not* like my dad," she begins. To her, the division of acceptable and unacceptable traits was all very clear: "I wanted to marry somebody like my dad who I saw as calm, smart, strong, personable, sociable, political, thoughtful. Somebody who was an incredibly take-charge guy. People always gravitated to him." She describes how her father, a college professor, always had a bevy of admiring students and former students, young people who would continue to call him and drop by years after they had graduated from the college where he taught.

"On the other hand, when I looked at my parents' relationship I saw my dad as being far more dominant. I didn't really appreciate my mother's strengths, I think, until after my father died. And I was not going to be my mother in a relationship. So I really kind of married my mom. I mean I married a wonderful man who is very smart. But I feel like in a lot of ways I'm the stronger person in this relationship." Looking back, now that her father is no longer casting his long shadow over her marriage, Lillian sees how her marriage is lacking. "I was not drawn to him out of any passion," she says. The question of whether she can find satisfaction in her marriage is still open. Whatever happens now, she knows that it has to happen between herself and Matt.

Pain and Anger

Of course, many relationships will experience a similar—and likely temporary—disruption when a father dies. Even when our partnerships are built on solid grounds of mature love and clear-sighted perception of who we are and who our mates are, we may run into problems. For a while, even when this is not the norm for us, our fathers may become more important to us than our spouses. We may feel ill at ease and unhappy in our relationships, missing our fathers' presence and seeking them in our mates, in our surviving family members, and in ourselves. Particularly during the early stages of mourning, this longing may cause us to see problems in an otherwise stable relationship. Sometimes, in our grief, we may cause disruptions where before they did not exist. We may push our loved ones away, for example, and put distance between ourselves and our chosen partners. Sometimes we are simply so involved in our own grief that we have little emotional energy to spare. Although intellectually our partners recognize what we are going through, they may also feel abandoned as we mourn and, at times, revert from the women they love into lost little girls who miss their daddies.

"My husband has had to roll with the punches," acknowledges Jacqui, who describes herself as still sad and still depressed a year after her father's death. His death, and the deaths of several uncles and aunts that preceded it, has frightened her, she admits. "We're next in line," she says, "and that's scary." While she now emphasizes the importance of her child in her life, she also admits that she's shaken. Mortality has never seemed so real before.

Our withdrawal may be more direct as well. We may find ourselves backing off from intimacy, fearing the pain to which closeness makes us vulnerable. "I was just too afraid to be close to anyone then," says Thea, who left her longtime lover immediately after her father's death. "I just hurt too much to be near anybody. I shut down, or I picked fights with people," she recalls. In retrospect, her behavior at the time does not make her proud. "I wasn't present," she says. "I just shut down as a person."

As embarrassed as she may be about her past behavior, Thea shouldn't feel alone, the experts say. "The shock wave of such a loss just calls forth a host of very painful, very intense, and very conflicted feelings," says psychologist Froma Walsh. "The pain of loss is so great that a daughter may distance from another man in her life in wanting to protect herself from the pain of another loss."

Displaced anger at our fathers may also separate us from our partners. Guilt, too, the hopeless guilt that comes with the knowledge that it's too late to make amends, can twist us into pushing against love and sympathy, creating a chain reaction of thought that social worker Carol Tosone describes as: "Father is gone, I don't deserve to be happy. I don't deserve to be in a relationship." Such a turmoil of emotions may also cause us to lash out at those closest to us, and if a partner has in some way adopted the role of a departed father, how much more natural is it, then to pound on him or her. Indeed, for many of us in permanent relationships, the problems that arise at this time may tell us more about our unresolved conflicts with our fathers than about our relationships with our partners.

This can be tricky, because at first the problems may seem identical to those issues that depend solely on the relationship. It is only with some digging that our motivations became clear. For Lori, whose father died eleven years ago, the year immediately following this loss nearly saw the breakup of her marriage as well, "My husband and I started to have some issues, some really major fights," she recalls. Part of what was bothering her, she admits, was his apparent unwillingness to support her as she felt a spouse should. "I felt like he just wasn't being there for me, and I really needed him to be there."

Her husband suggested counseling. She resisted, but luckily he insisted, and once they were meeting with a therapist Lori discovered that her neediness predated the marriage. She found that she was really reacting to what she had wanted from her father as a child rather than what she needed from her spouse. "I ended up staying on in therapy and he sort of bowed out," she says. "Because clearly the issue was me and my father."

Where do the pangs of mourning end and the deeper issues of trust and care that underlie our marriages and partnerships begin? At what point do we separate the succor we seek from our partners from the lifelong support we expected as our birthright from our fathers? These lines can only be drawn by the individual and, in most cases, if we are being completely honest with ourselves, we will recognize some overlap as expectations old and new combine in fresh sadness and anger. The problems are as complex as our lives, but the connections between them—the overdetermined nature of our reactions to our partners and our fathers—may be useful to us. For although our feelings of distrust, discomfort, and distance may be temporary reactions to grief—stages in our mourning that our relationships will weather with time—they may also clue us in to our own deeper feelings toward commitment. Because it may not be until we have lost our fathers that we finally get to test the relevance of Freud's theory that daughters ultimately seek to marry their fathers. Whether we have, in fact, done so, or whether we ever wanted to, now that he is gone we face the evidence that he may have loomed larger in our personal cosmography than we had previously admitted.

It all seems so embarrassingly simplistic that it's difficult to confess, but nearly a hundred dollars in rental and late fees serve as undeniable evidence: I don't think I ever knew how much of a romantic hero my father was to me until I realized that at some level I was trying to replace him with Clint Eastwood. This wasn't a direct one-on-one correlation. I don't know how well I'd ever thought my father could have worn those dusty leather boots, and how much of that longing had always gone unfulfilled. Death puts an end to all the possible scenarios, all the heroism we hoped for, and what I lost may have been an equal, if uneasy, mix of real, protective Daddy and unrealized fantasy. But both disappeared with his death, forcing me to confront what I had wanted as well as what I had perhaps once had.

It's this duality of memory that we all must deal with, a death of expectations that clouds and confuses our more physical loss. However, when these ghosts have surfaced and have been dispersed, we have the unique experience of seeing our existing relationships with a fresh eye. Finally we may be able to realize what we have been working toward, or what demon we were reacting against. For those of us in long-term relationships, it's an opportunity to see what we have and also, perhaps more clearly than before, what we are lacking.

For many women, this crisis serves as a wake-up call. We may realize not only that we have been in relationships for reasons that no longer apply, but that we are now freed from the compulsion that bound us there originally. This does not have to mean dissolution of our relationships, however. How we choose to use this new clarity depends on many factors. For example, although we may have been bound by outdated compunctions, we were rarely completely limited or defined by them. Our fathers may have helped set our childhood ideals of love and commitment (or sent us into rebellion) and we may only now be discovering how great a factor their influence has been on some of our major life decisions. But we are no longer children, and as adults other factors—our age, our friendships, our social environment, even the years spent developing the patterns and grooves of our unions—have had some impact on who we now are and what we now want as well. Our newfound vision, therefore, may provoke a great range of reactions, any of which may be appropriate to our situation.

If we committed ourselves to someone as a reaction—primarily to please our father or to escape him—this is the time when many of us chose to opt out, as Thea did and as Marcy is considering. We may follow the lead of women like Rikki, who separated from her husband when she realized how her marriage was based on inappropriate and outdated notions, and then reestablished the relationship on a more equal ground. Or we may find that turmoil in our marriages truly reflects the roiling emotions within ourselves, a symptom of unresolved issues and a clue that we need to reexamine the relationships that we had with our fathers, not our partners. Clearly all of these reactions may be justified, any of them at any given time may be the most appropriate, the healthiest move for us and for our hopes for future happiness. Not all relationships are made to last.

Healthy Relationships

Nor do all crises extract such a high price. For many women, the loss of a parent may even help a partnership. Sometimes, to be honest, our parents were overinvolved in our relationships. Whether they loved our mates or continuously disapproved, our fathers may have interfered, and although that interaction leaves its own messy aftereffects, we may be better able to heal our partnerships once the parents are gone. In lesbian relationships, for example, the couple's sexuality may have become a "red herring" for all the extended family's troubles, acting as the focus for every issue. In what Professor Joan Laird (in *Lesbian, Gay, and Bisexual Identities in Families*) calls the "don't tell your father, it would kill him" scenario, the couple served as the source of all the family problems, a situation that placed a ridiculous stress on the two partners—and which will be recognizable to many straight women as well.

In cases where a daughter served as a principle caregiver and the illness had been extended, the father-daughter interaction may have eaten up resources of time and energy. When her father dies and when her mourning has passed its first, necessarily selfish stages, such a woman may be at liberty once again to give to the relationship as she hadn't in months or years. Then the investment of support given and accepted can strengthen a partnership. As the grieving lessens, the memory of crises survived together can be reassuring, proof for the couple that they can deal with life's troubles.

"After Dad died, I finally felt like my husband and I could get on with our own life together," says Wendy. "Because throughout our relationship we were dealing with my dad's cancer and subsequent depression. But I felt guilty for that at the same time, for being relieved that we did not have to face that anymore. For the first couple of years following Dad's death, I felt guilty for having any kind of fun, knowing that he could not enjoy the things we were enjoying, and that my mom was suffering at home all alone. My husband was very supportive and understanding. I felt closer to him for all that he had done for my family and me."

"My husband was very good about everything, and I mean it was tough," recalls Marcy, whose father suffered a sudden, massive heart attack and never resumed consciousness. In addition to her own shock and grief, she explains, as the oldest child she was called on to coordinate all the family travel arrangements, duties for which she was unprepared. "We had to travel back to another state for the funeral, and we had to cope with all these people coming together and trying to make plans—I have a big family. He was very helpful with everything. I really appreciated that."

To some extent, her husband temporarily accepted an almost parental role, guiding and advising Marcy through a crisis for which she was completely unprepared. "I had never gone to a funeral before. I had no idea what to expect," she recalls. "And he walked me through everything, which was very good. I guess things like that do bring you closer."

Marcy's story, showing how a healthy relationship can bend and grow to accommodate its member's changing—and sometimes temporary—needs, is not unique. Many times, in fact, a loss like the death of a father can enrich a couple's lives and allow both members of the relationship to discover new strengths and new ways of behaving. Gayle, for example, had always been the caregiver in her decade-long partnership with Louise; she'd always been the one who made the difficult major decisions about money and moving, and the one who was strong when a pet became ill or a good friend picked a fight. It took the death of her father to show her that she could relax and let Louise assume control sometimes.

"I let her take care of me in a way that I hadn't been able to before," she says. "It was a change in our relationship, and it made us more truly partners. For me, it was about trust, about letting someone take care of me. It let me grieve, and it brought me closer to her in a lot of ways, and then we didn't want to go back to the unevenness of before."

The classic Freudian model declares that we seek to marry our fathers. But speaking to women who are in permanent relationships and who have lost their fathers reveals a more homey truth: that perhaps it is not until we lose our fathers that we can see clearly who we have chosen for our mates. This, finally, is when we can move beyond our childhood needs or early antipathy and recognize our partners as colleagues and cohorts, people like ourselves to whom we turn for support, and with whom we may learn to weather the crises that life brings us.

CHAPTER 7

Babies and Mortgages

When we lose a parent, we move up a step in the generational hierarchy. Whether we considered ourselves children before, we are certainly adults now as our generation becomes the older generation. When we lose a father, specifically, we lose the parent who for many of us embodied security, often in the most material sense. And while there is no way to compensate for this loss, many of us refine our needs for family and home in response. Whether we are filling in the absence, or simply repositioning ourselves in our new roles as the heads of our own families, we often seek at this juncture to put down roots. For whatever reason, this is a period when many of us choose to have children or to buy houses, to bring living creatures into our lives and to settle into our communities in ways that we may not have been able to before.

Memorializing

For me, permanence is in the writing. Silly as it seems for someone who has spent much of her professional life working for newspapers, journals that after a day or a week are relegated to the litter box or the recycling bin, to me the recording of life in even a transient manner is a way of preserving it. When my father was dying, my first reaction was to write. I wanted to capture him as he had been, vital and strong, and the speed with which he was coursing through his life's latest phase, one of vulnerability, spurred me to write about that as well. Late at night, when my daily work for the paper was finished, I stayed at my desk, composing the essays that begin earlier chapters of this book. This was my way of shoring up the dam against time, against the flood of approaching grief. Despite the fragile, disposable nature of the medium in which I worked, I believed that somehow the words printed on that yellowing newsprint would hold against the tide, would somehow remain, if not in fact then in memory—in the minds of somebody who had read what I had written and understood. And when I realized that instead of stopping my father's death I was actually documenting it, I let that purpose take me over. Like any historian, carving my story into stone or into the minds of listeners at the agora by piling on the words, placing sentences upon sentences, I sought to build an edifice that would encapsulate memory. I sought, through writing, permanence, to grab immortality in the face of the looming mortality that threatened my father and, by example, all of my family.

A quick browse of bookstore shelves or contemporary journals reveals that I am not alone and that, in fact, in contemporary fiction, the loss of a father has come to be a rite of passage, akin to losing one's virginity or moving out of the family home. "We are all children until our fathers die," says a character in Melissa Bank's bestselling novel, *The Girl's Guide to Hunting and Fishing.* That's a feeling I wrote about, too.

All the reactions I went through I found echoed in fiction and memoirs. Again and again in such books, young women find themselves changing and growing, spurred on by the loss of their male parents. The death of the protagonist's father in Bank's novel facilitates her leaving a job she dislikes and ending an unsatisfactory relationship, changes many of us have experienced. Similar growth occurs in Marcy Bradshaw, the fictional heroine of Anna Maxted's novel, *Getting Over It*, after her father dies, and thus this novel may be seen as the direct descendent of the nonfiction essay Maxted wrote about her own father's death for *Cosmopolitan* UK. Indeed, the death of a father may be becoming the contemporary fictional marker for young women's coming of age, perhaps particularly as authors who have experienced these changes realize the desire to record them.

Even when we do not write directly about how our fathers' deaths affect our lives, we share the urge to remember and record, liberated from earlier restrictions. "Since he died, I feel free to write about him and me," agrees Australian novelist Carmel Bird. "If he were alive, I would find this more difficult." Bird's memories of her father, who died nearly ten years ago, preface a collection of stories, *Daughters and Fathers*, that she edited for the University of Queensland Press. "I can write about my love for my father more freely now than I could before," she says. "It's also kind of more important to do so. Maybe I keep him alive by writing this."

When we write, we memorialize our fathers—capture, before their essence leaves our memories, the best and worst of them, their quirky endearing traits and cold rejections. We can also explore issues that haven't been resolved by our fathers' passing by playing them out on paper. We can discuss topics left unmentioned while our fathers were alive and complete arguments left off years before in tears and frustration. For many of us, this is how we sort through the detritus, the grief and the anger, to find what has been left. When we write, we make something concrete out of our conflicting emotions. Most of all, when we write, we create something that brings back that which has been lost.

The urge to record—to give immortality to a person or a set of memories—is a natural response to death. For many of us, our first urge is to memorialize and dissect the past. For others, a more primal response to death is to look forward, to be proactive. These are the women who choose to bring new elements into their lives, who choose, unconsciously, often enough, as they respond to previously absent urges, to procreate or dig a garden. They are the future-oriented women.

We may, of course, experience both sets of responses. Both, after all may be reactions to the same motivation. Just as we, the writers and analysts, may need to dig through the past, to understand it, before we can put it to rest, so too may the family builders and home settlers be responding to early memories, rebuilding in physical terms what their fathers, or their parents as an intact unit, meant to them.

For me, as for perhaps many of the writers whose accounts I've read, what matters is the remembering, the interpreting that allows us to air our feelings and incorporate them into the body of our work. For others, women who express themselves without words, this new stage of life must be furnished in other ways, no less significant and often just as closely tied to the trauma, loss, and confusion of death. For many women looking at life beyond their fathers, the building of a family—no matter how unusual its components—is the most natural reaction to grief, pitting new life against death.

Welcoming New Life

The classic reaction, one documented recently in a doctoral dissertation presented at Brandeis University, is for women who have lost their fathers to want to bear a child. In her study of fifty single women who chose to have babies, researcher Faith Ferguson found that the death of a loved or important older person was a significant motivator, perhaps even the deciding factor for approximately 20 percent of the single mothers in her study. Among those women were many who had lost their fathers. "There were a number of women who said, 'When my father died, I decided I really do want to do this, and I really want to do this *now*,' " says Ferguson. This reaction gives us what experts refer to as a replacement relationship. Although both men and women may seek such substitutes after a loss, it is typically women who find it in parenting a child. (Men, say experts such as Froma Walsh, more commonly look for their replacement in another adult, perhaps by having an affair.)

For Gayle and her partner Louise, the deaths of both their fathers within eighteen months of each other were the catalysts in their decision to have a child together. For Gayle, who has always thrown herself into her work as an engineer, this was a complete turnaround. "I never really had a biological clock," Gayle says. "I never wanted children; I never thought I'd be good at it. Louise felt differently, but I was pretty adamant."

For Louise, the desire to have a baby increased exponentially after her father's death, and when Gayle's father also passed away, after a brief battle with lung cancer, Gayle found her earlier conviction wavering. They agreed to raise a child together and, because of fertility issues, Gayle donated the egg that Louise is carrying. Even beyond the basic biology, this is clearly their baby—a child they both want. "This is very far from where I thought I'd be," says Gayle, who at thirty-seven sees her life's focus shifting dramatically. "It's so clear to me that this is what Louise needs to do now, and it's so clear to me that we're supposed to be doing this together."

Of course, a great many factors play into our decisions about bearing and raising children. For many of us age is a precipitating factor. Many of us are in our later childbearing years when we lose our fathers. Those of us in our late thirties or early forties, for example, may have already found the question of motherhood pressing, as our fertility declines and the risks that accompany pregnancy increase. Many of us may in fact have decided to have children at this age no matter what other factors were involved, with time simply bringing together our biological deadline and the increasing likelihood of our father's dying. The proximity of these two life-changing events, therefore, may be somewhat coincidental.

What is different, however, is the emphasis on family. For women like Gayle, who had not felt a pull toward motherhood, the loss of her father seems to relate directly to her willingness to be a parent. "Family does feel more important now," she says, considering her family of origin, four siblings all older than she is. "I'm the youngest, and we're all dying off. So Louise and I are re-creating family," she says.

The pull may reveal itself in other ways, perhaps as one factor in a complicated decision. Marcy, for example, waited ten years after marrying to have her first child, but got pregnant with her second child right after her father died. Although she says her decision wasn't consciously thought out, she does believe the loss of her father played a role. "He was very family oriented," she says. Growing up with seven siblings, she said, she was always aware of her father's involvement with children, of his great love for large families. "He was very involved in everything, from diapering to bottles. He was the one up in the middle of the night a lot. And he always just stressed that it was important to put the children first before anything. That always stuck with me."

Along with the other factors, the awakening effect of death—the "carpe diem" reaction—cannot be discounted. The will toward life is strong, and repeatedly I hear women talking of a renewed zest for living, a fresh appreciation of our flesh-and-blood realities in reaction to their losses. In addition, often the deaths of our fathers change our lives in practical ways; while some women are newly burdened with care of their mothers or other relatives, many others report inheritances of land or money that allow them to assume new responsibilities. Such an inheritance, for example, may make raising a child possible, or at least more appealing. Again, these changes are the result of many influences. If you inherit the money to buy a house when your father dies, for example, we cannot say that your new purchase is proof that you associate your father with a home. However, it may lie behind your desire to invest in a home rather than a round-the-world trip.

This crisis brings us out of ourselves; it makes us reexamine life and family. Depending on who we are, we seek to remember and preserve, or we seek to expand our worlds. We may find ourselves desiring new love, new people, new babies to celebrate what has become newly dear to us in the aftermath of death.

Reinventing Family

Expanding one's family does not have to mean childbearing, however. Alternative families and options such as adoption and fostering are other ways we find to bring new life to our homes, particularly for those of us who are not in traditional relationships or who come from families that were not themselves traditional.

"I wanted to help children and I wanted to have a family. And whatever way that family came about was fine," recalls Ellen. Her father died as she hit forty, and she believes both her age and her loss helped change her priorities. Within three years of her father's death, she had bought a house and begun assembling her own version of a family. "Suddenly it was important. Not that I have a child and that I get married, but I wanted some kind of family."

For Ellen, that desire led her to explore adoption, particularly adoption of the older children who have more difficulty finding homes. While she learns more about the possibilities, she has become the foster mother to a young teen. She also began adopting "rescued" dachshunds, dogs that had been abandoned by their owners, and now has six of them running around the house and yard. The little "wiener dogs," as she fondly calls them, are a direct link to her father, who had kept them as pets when she was a very small girl.

As we talk, Ellen acknowledges another link between the family that she grew up in and the one she is now creating in her own home. Ellen herself was adopted, and she recognizes that the impetus to foster and adopt a child—particularly a child who is too old to be considered desirable by many prospective adoptive parents—both returns the favor and re-creates the family she once knew. In addition, Ellen recalls how, until her father died, the home he shared with her mother served as her "world headquarters," the place that friends could contact to find her after one of her frequent moves and the base she would return to after sojourns across Europe and Asia. Now that her father is gone, she finds herself building the same kind of secure base: a house, not an apartment; a place of stability for the children and pets she is welcoming into her life.

Between the house, her foster daughter, and her growing menagerie, Ellen's life has become significantly more rooted than it was in previous years. "Ten years ago, I lived overseas," she remarks, looking back at the changes her life has gone through. "Now, if I decided to leave for a year and travel the globe, I really couldn't. But it came naturally. It evolved."

As Ellen's extended family illustrates, the drive to nurture and to bring more life into our homes is not limited to children. Many of us find ourselves drawn to new pets or other living things after we lose our parents. Nor is this development limited to childless women, as Jacqui, who has a young son, found out.

"We just got a cat," she says, a little amazed at this development in her life. "I have not had a pet since I've been an adult, and that change, I think, is part of this family thing. My son, of course, was the momentum for wanting a pet. But something happened to me, too. For the first time in twenty-odd years I've been willing to actually have a pet. My family has shrunk, and I think that's why I've finally opened to the idea of taking on a pet."

Jacqui believes that the adoption of a kitten is clearly a substitute in her life, but one that she is willing to accept. "We have only one child and haven't had a second even though we would have liked to. So adding a pet . . . it's not a child, but it is another little person who needs caring. In a way it's like another member of the family, another little person around the house who requires my attention and affection."

In various ways, many of us refill our lives with family of our own making, often looking beyond traditional bonds and living arrangements in our search for warmth and fulfillment on our own terms.

Sylvia, for example, tells of how she went from virtually no family of her own to a houseful after an adult niece rented a room from her and she also offered shelter to a friend in transition who needed a place to live. "We still have our own separate lives, but it's satisfying to me," she says.

As with Ellen, the changes in Sylvia's life began with a desire to set down roots, to have a place that was truly her own. "Right after my father's death, I became determined to have a house, a house with a garden," remembers Sylvia, who was able to buy a home for herself a few years after her father died. What she sought in the aftermath of loss, she explains, was to "have a place that I can make my own, where I can create my own space and have an ongoing relationship with the surroundings.

"I feed the birds every day. I plant things and watch them bloom," she continues. By doing so, Sylvia brought life back where there had been desolation. She also reconnected with a side of her father that she had lost touch with, the part of him that also loved the land and the cycles of nature. He worked the small Midwestern farm she grew up on, she recalls, and often he would stay out in his fields long after dark, more for pleasure than out of necessity.

Now, digging in the dirt of her own New Jersey garden, even as the summer twilight fades, she feels close to her father. She understands what motivated him, remembering how "when my mother would be calling him into dinner he would just say, 'One more round!' And he would go around the fields on the tractor again. It was, in some ways, a sense of enjoying something so much that you don't want to quit."

As all these women point out, these changes—whether of putting down roots, finding love, or rediscovering a simple joy—may have come about naturally in the course of time. Even without the loss of a father, many women buy homes, have children, and find peace in a garden. Such discoveries may, indeed, be a normal part of our path through adulthood as we progress through our twenties, thirties, and forties. However, even if we would have made these changes in the ripeness of time, what we see here is the urgency, the call to settle down, to reproduce, to surround ourselves with life and with love.

Georgia, for example, does not doubt that she would have married her long-term boyfriend and bought a house—eventually. But in the months following her father's death, she found herself craving that feeling of being settled, particularly in regard to having a house of her own.

"I felt that I needed to figure out who I am and get settled. I suddenly felt like I needed to do all this stuff, because I didn't know how long I was going to be here. I guess it was facing mortality. But I just felt like, I really need to achieve my goals."

Healthy Models

Freed at last from the conflicts we may have experienced with our fathers, changes such as these reveal another side of our relationships with our parents. Did our fathers represent home to us, causing us to seek to re-create the stability we associate with them by buying houses or digging gardens? Did they represent family, compelling us to add children or other living creatures to our daily lives? Do we want most to treasure our memories of them as individuals or for the roles they played in our families, and do we now rush to memorialize or to communicate with them through our art?

Just as many of us who sought relationships unsuccessfully during our fathers' lives may have been able to relax into them when our fathers had died, so too many of us who craved the security and stability of our families of origin are now able to achieve these states. We can make the commitment to a child—or to a mortgage. We can be honest in our writing. We can be, finally, the adults. And as we step up to the plate, so to speak, into our new maturity, we often find ourselves desiring the things and the connections that made our parents seem adult to us: the house, the yard, the children.

In a way, we are all seeking a counterbalance. We have been thrown to some degree by the removal of our fathers, and we automatically reach out for that which will set us right. But what do we reach for, and what can it tell us about our interaction with the parent who has died? I remember once more laying the speaker wire for the sound system in the first apartment I shared with Jon, who is now my husband. It still makes me sad, in a bittersweet kind of way, to look around me at the house we now live in, at shutters I stained and he mounted, and to hear the slow "cluck" of the clock we bought together for the kitchen wall. I know that, for me, father meant capability, meant competence in practical matters, and a painstaking care that I have not yet been able to learn. But without him here, I have gotten a little more careful over time, measuring before I cut and marking before I drive the nail in. In this way, if no other, I am building a home based on the one I remember. It is not as neat; there are irregularities in the row of hooks or the shelves that hold our numerous books. But it feels warm and safe, quiet enough to work in, and that's the best of what I remember. That's what I want to take with me.

CHAPTER 8

Mothers
and Daughters

Most of us will lose our fathers before we lose our mothers, and this means that with our fathers' deaths another relationship will change: the one we have with our widowed mothers. In some ways, this changes everything about the mother-daughter connection. The parent we are left with, our mother, has perhaps shifted from one of a two-parent team to become an unattached woman. She is still our mother, but she may now also be a woman alone. She is often single and independent, but may also be vulnerable as she reconfigures her own life. For many of us, an unexpected benefit of this period comes from our improved, more equal relationships with our mothers, while others watch old tensions spring up without our fathers' modifying influence. For still others, increased responsibility toward mothers becomes a reality.

Communications

"Dear girl," the message on my answering machine began. "Don't look for any e-mails from me today. My computer has died." My subsequent phone call elicited more information. "It sounded like HAL in *2001*," she said, letting her voice flatten into a machine-like calm: " 'My brain is going.' Pffft." All of which explained the necessity for the voice message, something of an aberration in the normal routine between my mother and myself, and the beginning of a daylong odyssey that pretty much captured our relationship.

First of all, the e-mail. While I knew that my mother used the service to keep up with several far-flung friends and with my aunt (being of the generation that still considered long-distance phone calls a luxury), I also suspected that I, less than two miles away, was her primary correspondent. This was largely due to the parameters that I had established a few years before, my attempt to balance the closeness she desired with the distance I needed, and most of the time it worked perfectly. I was her only truly responsive child, the only close family member she had left with whom to bounce the day's events around. With e-mail, she could zap me a message about a story in the day's paper, a fight with a friend, or the hawk she saw occasionally lazily circling above the sky-lit pool where she regularly swam laps. "Do you think it sees us as salmon?" she would muse electronically. "Do you think it fantasizes about swooping down and carrying one of us off?"

With such thoughts confined to my computer screen, to be read and responded to when I chose to take a break from whatever else I was doing, the relationship worked for me. For reasons that most adult daughters will understand, I was as leery of encroachment upon my own, adult life as I was of complete disconnection, and the e-mail updates reassured me. When I checked in, as I usually did at least once a day on weekdays, I saw a woman who had survived her husband's long, miserable decline and death with her self intact, a woman who took care of her health and her mind, and whose social life was more varied and often busier than mine. And also, although I didn't like to admit this to myself, a woman who was often lonely, an only child who had been married almost all of her adult life and who had lost two of her three children to death and debilitating illness. When I sensed that loneliness welling to uncomfortable proportions I would call her and be rewarded. "Dear girl, it's lovely to hear your voice," she would say, and I would tell myself I was imagining the trace of a reprimand in the reminder that it had been a while. And there would be times when I would call her for myself, wanting the comfort of my mother, a woman of another age who would protect me no matter what, and who would still offer to "sprechen" me against the evil eye. I never could tell how seriously she took the counterspell she recited in Yiddish, spitting three times after each repetition, but I knew it did me good. Someone was looking out for me.

I wanted to do the same for her, particularly now that she had a specific problem. I also was in the midst of a good writing run, the kind where you look up hours later, breathless with the knowledge that you've captured something ineffable in words, and wanting nothing more than to dive in again. Still, she was my mother, and despite her computer literacy, she was of another generation. So after our phone conversation about her unresponsive computer, I told her to call the store where we'd purchased her grape iMac. I thought she might still have a service contract, and told her that I'd help transport the small but unwieldy machine there later that afternoon. Then, my concentration broken anyway, I went out to meet a friend for lunch and to do some errands that I had postponed while still in the creative thrall. Upon my return, three phone messages greeted me, each detailing another stage of the process. "Dear girl, it seems I no longer have a service contract, but they do have a service department. If you would help me bring it in, I would be most grateful." Click. "Dear heart, you're still not home, so I'm going to just run it over myself. Love and kisses." Click. "Dear girl. The computer seems to have grown heavier in the last year. If you're still offering it, I would deeply appreciate your help." Click. I felt the familiar combination of guilt and annoyance growing in me, although my rational mind reminded me that each message made sense and that none had reprimanded me for my two-hour absence during what was, to her, a major technological crisis. I thought of her age, which she would hate, and her relative inexperience with computers, which she would admit. And I remembered my own hopelessness and frustration when, two weeks earlier, I had somehow frozen my new laptop, and the fumbling statements I had made, panicked to the point of computer illiteracy, to the company's tech support person. And then I kicked myself. And called her back.

"Hi, it's me," I said, probably needlessly, when she answered my call. "I'm thinking you should try calling Apple tech support."

"But it won't even turn on," she protested, making what I had to agree was a valid point.

"Yes, but it's free, and if they can figure it out, then you don't have to give up your machine for a week." Plus, I can get back to work, I thought. Dubiously, she agreed and I gave her the number that had pulled my laptop out of the deep freeze not that long before. "Just try them. If they can't do it, call me back and we'll bring the beastie down to the CompuStore."

I didn't hear from her for an hour, and I tried calling her. The line was busy. I went back to work, but found I couldn't concentrate. I tried her again, and the line still pulsed with that annoying busy honk. I turned my attention to a lesser assignment and got a little work done before trying again. Busy. I went out to grocery shop. When I returned, of course, a message awaited me. "Dear girl, I am triumphant!" Her voice trumpeted her pride. "I'm now reloading software, and all seems to be well." Four hours with tech support, it turned out, had located the faulty program that had indeed crashed her system. With several experts consulting, my mother had gotten her computer back up and running and was in the process of downloading the programs for the word processor and e-mail that she used every day, as well as her CD-ROM of the Louvre and the radio software that allowed her to listen to her favorite New York classical station. She'd managed to communicate with computer experts, and she's had the perseverance and patience to do the necessary inputting. At an age at which many of her contemporaries were retiring to smaller worlds and increasing dependency, she had tackled and conquered a new field of knowledge. I was immensely proud of her. And my day's work had still been thrown off course. Another day in the life of adult daughters and their widowed mothers.

New Competencies

Much has been written about mothers and daughters, about the interplay of intimacy and frustration that marks this singular and often symbiotic relationship. Our mothers were the first parent we knew, and they are women, like us. For good or ill, we are too often too involved with our mothers to be able to happily regulate the distance between us, and for many of us the pursuit of this balance can be a lifelong quest. What we do not often examine, however, is how that relationship changes when we lose our fathers. How a triad relationship, that of two parents to a child, develops into a dyad, of mother to daughter, and can evolve further over time to a relationship of woman to woman, or, perhaps inevitably, dependent elder to caregiving adult.

It is a relationship most of us will come to know. Given the relative life spans of women as compared to men, more of us will see our mothers survive our fathers. Most of us will have extended relationships with our mothers after we lose our fathers. For many of us, according to a 1991 study led by Rosalind Barnett, our relationships with our mothers will be the longest lasting of our lives.

It's an important connection. Overwhelmingly, adult daughters find themselves increasingly involved in their mothers' lives after their mothers are widowed, Barnett and her fellow researchers reported in an article for the *Journal of Marriage and the Family*. In part, that is because once our mothers are widowed, we become increasingly significant to *their* lives. While we may have enjoyed a period of distance during our adult years, once our mothers are widowed the bond becomes tighter, the interaction closer, as we take on tasks and satisfy companionship needs for our surviving parents. "When only one parent is alive, the adult daughter plays a more important part in fulfilling parental needs," concluded Barnett. In lieu of our fathers, we are the ones called upon for conversation and company, in times of trouble, and when decisions involving health and property must be made. Much of this seems a natural, an organic shift. We are family, after all. For many of us, caring for our mothers is part of a final compact we had with our fathers, to take care of their wives, our mothers. This is a role that is increasing over time as we, their competent adult children, the ones who followed our fathers out into the world with careers and independence, fulfill not only the traditional daughter role of family caregiver but also the expected son role, taking over the father's duties at his death.

As Rita recalls, the knowledge that she would accept responsibility for her mother allowed her terminally ill father to relax as he died. He'd been increasingly restless, she remembers, in a way that had nothing to do with his pain medication or diminishing hours of consciousness.

"He finally asked me what he could do," says Rita. "He was worried that my mom wouldn't be able to handle it. And I told him that I would take care of her. That was pretty much the last he spoke; he died a few hours later. Once he knew that that was taken care of, I think he was able to let himself go."

This kind of role-swapping tends to be easier to implement with our mothers than with our fathers. It may continue a familial role of subordination for our mothers, particularly since many older women may have assumed a nearly childlike incompetence and dependency during their marriages. Although the conventional split in responsibilities often left women in charge of the complicated running of a home, their lack of experience in handling decisions about the outside world may have left them fearful of sudden independence.

At times, our mothers may look to us for direction. Sometimes that can mean helping our mothers learn tasks that our fathers routinely performed for years, as when Ellen taught her mother how to handle health insurance and other financial forms. At other times, we may find ourselves pushed into almost parental roles, permanently assuming duties that our mothers seem too timid to take on despite their physical and mental competency, or donning emotional mantles that may be inappropriate to our relative age and experience.

"I feel like I took over my father's role," complains Lucy. "Like, my father took care of her, now I'll have to take care of her. I'm the more pragmatic one," she explains. "My mom's an artist. She's dreamy, and she's very smart, but she doesn't often show it. She bought a new car, and she had the car for two weeks, and the valet in the parking garage pointed out, 'Miss, Miss, the car has a scratch on it.' I felt sick. I felt so bad that her car was scratched because she really liked it. My sister finally told me that my mother had scratched the car herself, backing it into a pick-up truck. 'She didn't want you to know,' my sister told me. She treats me like the mom, and she was pleading with my sister: 'Don't tell Lucy! Lucy will kill me!' "

The price such dependence extracts from us may be a decreased respect for our mothers, particularly if we were what Patricia Reis calls "father identified," that is, if we patterned our lives on our more active, worldly fathers. Such fostered dependence may have been a useful habit for our mothers; in some ways, the prefeminist society encouraged it. But their continued acceptance of this subordinate position makes it difficult for us to regard them as mature, independent women. As a result, we often lose regard for our mothers and try to distance ourselves from them, and from the parts of ourselves that are like them. But when we try to dissociate ourselves from our maternal legacy, we lose a chance for real communication and closeness with our surviving parent. Plus, we shut ourselves off from a vital part of ourselves. Nor does our "help" necessarily do our mothers a service, since it perpetuates what may have been an assumed vulnerability, a learned helplessness that could, with proper support and encouragement, be unlearned. The situation serves nobody.

Not that our mothers are entirely responsible; a relationship is created by two people. However, we are often the ones who have the means at hand to change the relationship. In such cases when our mothers have been overly and needlessly dependent, we can use the looseness of the new situation, the shift in family dynamics that follows a loss, to change the patterns. At best, we can establish new paradigms; at worst, we can discover, through our attempts to communicate, how we feel and how much we are willing to give to certain roles.

It is important, at this point, to observe that not all of our widowed mothers share the same level of competency. Froma Walsh marks the difference between many of our widowed mothers, who are in their fifties, sixties, and seventies, and "old old," women in their eighties and above, or those with disabilities, who may be physically incapable of handling the responsibilities of living alone. For these women, aid may be given without condescension. But for younger widows, or fit and healthy women of any age, such assistance can be detrimental.

"Such women can develop new competencies," says Walsh, stressing that daughters can affirm their mothers' potential, encourage them to take on new tasks and venture into arenas where they have never tested themselves. "I have a friend who was widowed with two young adult children. Her husband died suddenly," says Walsh. "And she's now doing stocks online. She joined a club of women at middle age who are learning about the Internet and learning about investment. A daughter should encourage her mother to network with other women to develop those areas of competency." Having seen my mother tackle the Internet with a zest and growing fluency that many of my peers would do well to emulate, I can attest to the truth of Walsh's statement. Unless we want to, we never stop learning.

Accepting and encouraging our mothers' independence can be awkward for us, however. Particularly in the social arena, we are not usually accustomed to seeing our mothers as women. We knew them as our *mothers*, not as fellow adults who raised us, who worked in the house or out to keep a family together. We do not usually picture them as women like ourselves, as partners enjoying or leaving relationships, as people like us who have lived with the mixed consequences of their actions. Unless our mothers had been living alone for a long time before the death of our fathers, we tended to see them as part of a unit, as teamed with our fathers (or stepfathers or partners) in their roles as our mothers, and not as women. Now fate conspires to show us the other faces of our mothers, and makes this time full of discovery for us both.

For many of us, this can be an uncomfortable transition. If our mothers start dating, for example, we have to accept them as sexual beings. If we have not faced it before, we are now confronted with the reality that the tight parental unit—the monolith of support, discipline, and security that protected our childhood—was comprised of two humans, one of whom is now as single and lonely as we have ever been. Some of us may experience this discovery as a betrayal, what family therapists such as Terry Hargrave call "split loyalty." Usually, split loyalty becomes an issue in families after a divorce, when children—even adult children—may find themselves siding with one parent or the other. After the death of a parent, particularly a father, this split may be most pronounced when a widowed mother becomes sexually active again. As Hargrave illustrates: "I had one client whose father had been dead for two years, and she said, 'My mother's having an affair!' as if she were an adulterer. When I pointed this out to her it was a revelation. It was the first time that she had considered that her mother was not doing anything wrong."

Sometimes our discomfort grows from the shifting in roles between ourselves and our mothers. Instead of being the ones who were taught, protected, and advised about romance or dating, we may find ourselves cast in these "adult" roles, as our mothers turn to us for guidance. This can throw us further into the enabling, paternal role, amplifying our desire to treat our mothers as vulnerable. "It bothers me," admits Rita, talking about the possibility that her mother might date. For her, the issue turns immediately to her gullibility. "I worry about some guy who would end up helping my mom make choices that I didn't think were good for her. That would bother me. I don't think I'd really want to see her out with another guy." Rita means well, but clearly her discomfort with her mother is causing her to treat the older woman like a child.

If we try, at times we can balance the real vulnerability of our newly single mothers with respect for them as adults. "I sat my mom down and said, 'This is real. It's an epidemic,' " Greta recalls saying to her mother about AIDS. "I told her, 'you've got to use condoms.' "

No matter what our comfort level, this change can be an opportunity to re-create the relationship. With the family structure broken by mutual loss, we have a window of time in which we may, at best, be able to learn about our mothers as women, and let them into our lives as well.

For some of us, such as Raquel, the quiet of mourning offered a perfect opportunity for this rediscovery. "I remember saying to one of my friends, 'I just don't have a social life. All I do is hang out with my mother,' " says this otherwise social and sophisticated Los Angelena. "And she said, 'Well, maybe this is the time in your life where you're supposed to spend time with your mother because things change and you might not get another opportunity to have this kind of quality time with her.' And she was right, because now my mother's got this incredible social life. She's got a companion; we call him her boyfriend. They square-dance; they take waltzing classes and tango classes. She does that, and she teaches painting. She's got a really full life. And so do I.

"But the year that I lived with her, our whole relationship opened up. We talked about everything. We talked about sex, and we both talked about our sex lives. We became friends."

A Time of Growth

Such communication is easier when our mothers make a successful transition into a newly full and fulfilling life. Losing a spouse is widely considered the most stressful event of one's life, but for many women, once the initial grief has passed, the loss of a husband has also come to mean the loss of old and outdated proscriptions. For such women, unafraid to venture into the next phase of their lives, widowhood can be a time of self-discovery. Particularly when our parents' union was not a happy one, this period can be quite freeing for our mothers in ways that are difficult for us to imagine. It is easy to forget, for example, that our mothers came of age in an era of fewer options. Many of them stayed in relationships that we might have left, out of a sense of obligation or morality, or a fear of having nobody to rely on. Faced with no choice but to develop an independent life, these women may blossom.

Lita, for example, was extremely worried about her mother— and fearful of the responsibility that she thought she would have to take on as the elderly woman's caregiver. All through her father's final illness, she had been her mother's main support and, as an only child, she had taken care of her mother during the months afterward as she sank into near-catatonic helplessness. Finally, Lita made the decision to sell the suburban family house and move her mother into a retirement community near her own home on the East Coast. Her mother did not seem to care about the process, and accepted Lita's decisions in a childlike, helpless manner. Lita began to despair.

Six months later, Lita's mom, Lily, was a different woman. "She suddenly had this paradigm shift and became enormously positive," Lita recalls with continuing wonder. "Things happened that seemed incomprehensible to me about her because she and my father had both been such recluses. For example, she went on all the outings in order to meet people. And she's really happy."

After forty-five years of living in her husband's constricted world, Lily learned to branch out. "She's approaching a birthday, which will also be about the anniversary of when she came out here, and she said this past year has been the best year of her life—which is an amazing thing to say at seventy-nine."

Part of that new happiness, Lita acknowledges, is because in the retirement community Lily has found love. "She didn't have a very romantic relationship with my father for a really long time and she's now in the middle of one, and that really does a lot for somebody."

Reshaping Our Relationships

As our mothers reinvent themselves as single women and as widows, we have an unprecedented opportunity to reshape our relationships with them. We may be free to communicate in ways we previously ignored and tackle subjects that had been actively discouraged by our fathers or by the way our parents functioned as one unit. This opportunity comes with a burden. Particularly if our mothers are leaning on us for support or advice, we may need to consciously reconsider boundaries. Although many women have told me about the joyful rediscovery of their mothers, many have also told me about the reappearance of lifelong issues.

"She needed me to help her get the house and finances settled," recalls Marcy, whose stormy relationship with her mother came to a head in the months following her father's death. "But she also didn't want to burden me, the 'baby,' with details. And after all was said and done we had one time where we sat at the kitchen table and we talked about all of the tension. I think to my mother I was the competition for my father's attention. And we resolved a lot of that, or at least talked about it. I think I had a coming-to-terms with my mother."

Depending on the relationship between our parents, this may be the first time that we can communicate with our mothers without that sense of rivalry.

"There are still moments that are stressful, but there's much more communication now and much more support than there ever was," says Marcy. "There definitely are shades of the old relationship," she says. "It hasn't fully come around, but it's so much better than it was. And that's definitely something I've become very aware of since my father's death."

These issues may be aggravated if our fathers acted as intermediaries in the family, translating for us and our mothers. The challenge, then, is to grow beyond the old patterns and bridge the gaps left by our father's death.

"At the beginning, it seemed like we were constantly rubbing up against each other like two pieces of sandpaper," says Nina. Her mother is in her fifties and healthy. But even without the complications of aging and poor health, the two squabbled constantly in the months following their loss. Without Nina's father as a buffer, she and her mother have had to work out a way to successfully interact. "For the first time since I was probably eleven years old, I had to deal with my mother. I had to work out whatever is going on between us with her because I couldn't go running to my dad."

The birth of Nina's son brought the situation to a crisis. Her mother, always outspoken, began insisting on details (such as her preferred storage for a stroller) just when Nina was finding herself short on time, energy, and patience. She lost her temper, and the two had a screaming fight. But when things calmed down, Nina was able to initiate a discussion with her mother about their different approaches to life and to babies and their accouterments. In the ensuing talks, Nina let her mother know where and when her input would be appreciated and when Nina would always tell her to butt out. At first the conversations were painful; Nina felt disloyal and cold. But she is clear now that they were not only necessary, but also improved their relationship.

"I have had to learn to answer to the situation," she says. "Because when it's just the two of you, you can't avoid it. And I've really gotten to know her. I've had to, because I didn't have Dad around to do it for me."

At times, the new relationship may not be closer. If a relationship has been problematic, after all, a crisis is not likely to improve it. Usually we find ways to deal with each other; we accept the inevitability of family and work toward a truce. But sometimes the loss of our fathers also means the end of a reason to find any middle ground. This severing of ties may be most common with stepmothers, in particular stepmothers who came into our fathers' lives after our earliest childhood. In some such cases, although certainly not all, the death of a father also brings the end to the link that bound us to his wife or other partner of whom we had grown fond.

"We've always called her 'mom,'" says Jacqui of the woman who married her father when she was in her teens. "But it's become a little more clear that she's actually a stepparent now that my dad's gone. She's eighty years old now, and there's a tendency for an adult child to start taking care of older parents, but she's made it very clear that she is independent."

This is certainly the exception, rather than the rule. Many of us rely on families built through choice, rather than blood, and many women report close and enduring ties with women who also loved their fathers. But where the blood tie does not exist, perhaps other factors may have more weight. The jealousy that can build over a father's attention—the competitive aspect of the daughter-mother relationship that is usually absorbed into the deeper bonds of a healthy family—may come more into play when the tight mother-daughter bond does not exist. In addition, in families where the children may have already been on their way to adulthood, a new wife or partner may have seen herself more as the father's companion than as a surrogate mom, and this crisis may be a chance to shed an unwanted or ill-fitting role.

Whatever the motivation, although many women do report close and warm relationships with widowed stepmothers, several have told me of a disconnection when the person who had been their father's mate seemed disinclined to continue the relationship with her husband's children. The reasons for the failure of this relationship are difficult to sort out after the fact, and many other factors ranging from individual relationships with the stepparent and that person's age and health, only complicate the equation.

"When he was alive it was great and she was fine," recalls Georgia, whose father had remarried after his daughters were grown. "She was never a maternal figure for me, but we were very friendly. But there was an interesting twist after he died. She kind of turned against my sister and me and disowned us."

Trying to understand the hostility that flared up in the weeks following her father's death is difficult if not impossible. In Georgia's case, the intensive, nearly constant care that her father needed in his final illness certainly complicated the situation. In retrospect, her father's wife seemed to assume that many of the caregiving duties would be picked up by his adult daughters. Since Georgia and her sister both lived out of state, however, the primary burden fell on her father's wife, necessitating her early retirement from a job she loved.

"I think she was resentful that we hadn't spent more time with him, that we hadn't helped out even more. She had retired early to be his nurse. And I think she was just exhausted," says Georgia, looking back on the factors that probably led to their falling out. "When he died she kind of fell apart, I think, and she took a lot of her anger and frustration out on us." Despite efforts by Georgia and her sister to reconcile, even calling in family friends to mediate, the woman they had always considered a stepmother will not see them.

For Jacqui, the distance that her stepmother has begun imposing between them is felt most strongly at the holidays, which she had previously presided over with Jacqui's father. "I'm the one who is organizing Christmas now," says Jacqui. "I'm the center of the family." Jacqui explains her assumption of the hostess and cooking duties that her stepmother had fulfilled while her father was alive. "My stepmother said to me, 'You and your sister, you feel like orphans now.' That's the feeling and I'm trying to fill that void."

What Jacqui and her stepmother may be experiencing are the differences in what each expect of family roles and traditions, differences that had been subjugated to the wishes of Jacqui's father when he was alive. In retrospect, it seems that Jacqui's stepmother had adapted herself to her husband's wishes, cooking special holiday meals and hosting large gatherings, but at some level she did not feel invested in these traditions. Now she feels free to slough them off as unnecessary window dressing. Jacqui, to whom the traditions have deeper meaning, experiences this as abandonment. She is picking up the slack, fulfilling the familial role her stepmother no longer desires, but she cannot hide her hurt.

Some of the rejection Jacqui feels is aggravated by her stepmother's age. At eighty, her stepmother admits, she is looking to lighten her domestic load. Part of not wanting to host the family celebration comes down to not wanting to take on the necessary cooking and cleaning, and this is a change in her stepmother that Jacqui should be aware of and should respect.

This is a difficult juncture, with health and aging complicating a transition during which we may feel more in need of "mothering" than we have in years. We need to respect our own desires and encourage our mothers' autonomy; at the same time we must find what feels like an appropriate level of caring and interaction. It's a fine balance, one that sometimes calls on us to develop an emotional objectivity that we've never before needed.

Emotional Hangovers

Popular culture has idealized the mother-daughter relationship, sanitizing the often real conflicts into the stuff of light humor. Mothers and daughters are supposed to complain about each other's stubbornness. We're expected to fight, as long as by the last act we recognize how similar we really are and then kiss and make up. For many of us, this is not a tenable reality during most of our lives—until this point. What we have when we lose our fathers is often an opportunity to redefine the interaction between us, a last chance in which we can make everything right.

It would be doing all of us ornery, individual mothers and daughters a disservice to lie and say that this is an easy transition to make, or that our relationship will necessarily become more comfortable over time. Despite the light tone and very real love with which I opened this chapter, it is difficult for me to write about my mother, just as it remains difficult for me to sort out the emotional hangover from our last fight or the expectations I still harbor, fed partly by fantasy and partly by memories from a child-hood that was many years ago. That thorniness also springs from the very vitality of our relationship. She is alive and well as I write this, and therefore she is likely to read whatever I write. Because we are both alive, we are both still growing. Our relationship is constantly changing. At times, her health issues are magnified in my worries and my own denial about her aging, and reflected back. At other times, her concerns for me, for my husband, and for my work compel her to try to comfort or advise me more than I'd like, and when I pull back we both must try to recalculate and set a measured response against the primal hurt of rejection. We are separate people, nearly forty years apart in age and worlds apart in experience.

Never was that more clear than at my father's deathbed, or, to be more specific, in the elevator we shared every day from his hos-pital room to the lobby and the street.

That's when one of the traits my mother and I share compli-cated our interactions, making a difficult time even more so. At first, I was the one who made things harder, falling back on our shared favorite coping mode: a near stoic calm. The kind of auto-matic pilot that has gotten us through all the crises that have faced our family kicked in again during those final few weeks. At my father's bedside, we'd both appear in control, more or less. My mother would occasionally sniff into her handkerchief, but I know from friends' reports that my face was frozen in the lock of shock and dismay. I held this outer calm even as she'd try to comfort me.

"He doesn't mean it," I remember her telling me one after-noon, close to the end, as we rode down the elevator. My father had grown increasingly grumpy and, perhaps mercifully, increas-ingly disconnected from reality, and he had vented his mumbling spleen on me only moments before. "That's not really him talk-ing," she said, or words like it, reaching out to pet my arm. Rigid with feeling, I held myself still, thinking about the office I would have to face soon. I could not open myself to the hug she would have preferred. My rigidity, I believed in my core, was all that was holding me together.

I realized afterward that it was also keeping us apart, holding us back from finding comfort in each other. But I kept that still mask on for weeks. During our brief midday visits, I felt myself rendered incoherent by the rush of emotion and events. At night, I used the office and my burgeoning writing as an excuse to avoid her calls, to avoid the fear and need I would hear in her voice. Her husband had been ill for years, sleeping or drugged for much of his last months at home, but he had been present. Soon, he would not be.

Knowing the immensity of her loss, feeling a little guilty for my unresponsive state, it seemed natural to defer to her when it came time to plan the disposition of his remains. This time it was *her* inappropriate stoicism, her denial masquerading as pragma-tism, that nearly shipwrecked us both.

The process started fairly normally, at least for our family. My father hadn't wanted a religious service of any kind; my parents, both raised Jewish, had pretty much rejected any form of organ-ized religion throughout most of my lifetime. What he had asked for, what they both wanted, was cremation with the ashes dis-persed over the ocean. My father had chosen the artists' colony of Provincetown at the tip of Cape Cod, where he and my mother had spent many weeks of summer, for his final farewell, and although he died in January, we set out to honor that request.

"When shall I pick you up?," I remember her asking me. We'd been told by the funeral home that handled the cremation that we'd be able to have his ashes in two days.

"I don't think you should drive," I remember responding. I couldn't imagine a newly bereaved widow taking on this tiring task even if she was my indomitable mother. Plus, the forecast called for the nasty combination of sleet, snow, and cold driving rain that made New England so unpleasant through its darkest months.

"I'd be more comfortable driving," she said, or words to that effect, as we each pulled back and forth over the final farewell.

"I'd be happy to do it," I told her.

"My car is heavier, so its safer on the roads in bad weather," she responded. "I *want* to drive."

We went on like this for a while, and then I had a breakthrough.

"Look, neither of us is up for this," I finally said. "We're hiring a car and driver." She demurred. I held to my point, supporting my decision by reminding her of the forecast and of our fatigue. Ultimately, she gave in. Practically, rationally, it made sense for neither of us to drive, and that was what won my case. But of course this argument was simply cover; what I really wanted, in lieu of a proper funeral, was that one touch of formality. A suited limo driver and a black town car would lend a bit of ceremony to my father's farewell.

"This is silly," I remember her saying that morning, as the day opened even more miserable and wet than anticipated. "Don't you think the Charles River would serve as well?"

No, I told her, and then the limo arrived and we were on our way.

The hundred-mile drive, a quick commute in good weather, dragged on like purgatory that day, and as we sat, mostly silent, I grew increasingly glad that I had pushed for a driver. I knew that in our family mythology I was the "sentimental" one, the one who always got upset over leave-takings, the one who favored tradition over my parents's cooler, more intellectual views, although I have grown to suspect that my mother speaks on impulse as often as I. Either way, on this day neither of us were at our most rational nor in peak condition for a difficult drive, and as we made our slow way down the icy highway I congratulated myself on insisting on the limo. And, as well, that I hadn't let my mother toss what remained of my father in the slow, muddy river that meandered blocks away from their condo. She would have regretted it as well as I, one day, and by then my comfort would have been for naught.

When we got to Provincetown, however, my planning fell short.

"Excuse me?" The driver had rolled down the privacy window that separated our compartments. "Where exactly would you like to go?" My mother directed him to the stone jetty at the far west end of town. Extending out to a small lighthouse and barrier sandbar, the table-size blocks of granite had been a favorite stroll of my father's.

In sleeting rain, however, the uneven stone walk was another matter, complicated by the dress shoes my mother and I had both worn as part of our appropriately funereal attire. We started slipping as soon as we stepped onto the rocks, me holding my mother's hand, she holding the small cylindrical box that was my father.

"Excuse me, excuse me!" Our driver came running out of the parked car, holding a large umbrella and looking like he was almost willing to risk a frozen dunk to avoid losing his passengers. With his help we proceeded, very slowly, another few feet. The block ahead tilted at an angle that would have been fine for sneakers, in fine weather, and we gave up.

"Let's try the main dock," my mother suggested once we were back and warming up in the toasty car.

The level plank dock was slippery enough, but we managed to reach its end without incident despite our preoccupation: me looking around for officials who might try to stop what I'd learned was considered illegal dumping and my mother deep in her own thoughts. "Madeline said I shouldn't open it," my mother said to me, as we stood at the dock's edge. "It's not all ashes; there are chunks of bone, she said, and it's very disturbing." Whatever romantic image I had formed of wind-blown ash, I quickly squelched, and after a moment's silence I watched as she tossed the box up and out into the gray, choppy harbor. The day was not fated to go smoothly.

"It's floating!" my mother wailed, and sure enough, it was, tilted just a bit as it bobbed up and down on the wind-driven chop.

"There it goes. It's sinking; it's sinking." I lied through chattering teeth, as I took her arm and forced her to turn away from the buoyant little box. "Let's get some lunch."

That's when the value of the driver came into play, I realized, as she and I both opted for hard liquor after our drenching, difficult morning. If the drive out was quiet and tense, the trip back was silent—both of us drained almost beyond thought.

"I've just realized," I do remember her saying to me either during that interminable ride or in the numb days that followed. "You've lost your father."

In such stressful situations, we tend to turn inward, to focus on ourselves. The challenge in such a situation is to transcend narcissism, to recognize our individual crises. We had gone through the same set of events, but our experiences were utterly different. In so many ways, our responses were related—passionate, emotional, defensive—and in many ways these responses kept us apart. I was beginning to learn how individual we are, despite the complex relationship that bound us. It's a process of discovery that continues to this day.

As Our Mothers Decline

As I write this, my mother is healthy and fit, planning another of the long trips that have taken her around the globe and on which she has met several of the friends who now fill her days. Not all women, I know, are so fortunate. One of the sad realities of our new relationships with our mothers is that they may of necessity be brief. However ambivalent we feel about our mother's burgeoning independence, and how healthy it is for our mothers to rediscover themselves as competent women, we must realize that they are aging. If our mothers were young widows, the period of their independence might last for many years. For too many, however, the halcyon period is brief.

Wendy found herself helping her mother both emotionally and legally after a time of renaissance in which she and her mother reinvented their relationship on a more equal footing.

"My father had been ill for a long time," says Wendy, a young mother herself. "I wanted her to have a good time. And once she realized that I didn't have a problem with it, then she started opening up to me more."

Wendy experienced the common squeamishness that many daughters report, attributing her reaction not so much to the idea of her mother with another man as to the sudden switch in their roles. "She'd ask, 'What do you think of this? Do you think I should go out with him?' It was kind of funny," she says. "I'd get off the phone with her and have to sit there for a little while and think about it."

Still, both women made the transition well, reestablishing boundaries and keeping their senses of humor intact until her mother's new life went awry. The first crisis came about when Wendy learned that her mother's now live-in boyfriend was using her. Although her mother had been embarrassed to admit it at first, she began to confess to her daughter that her new beau was living off her money. When it came out that he had reneged on several agreements, such as to sell his business and invest the proceeds for them both, Wendy was enlisted to help her mother sever the relationship. This would have been difficult enough without complications, but in the middle of a legal proceeding to separate their bank holdings, Wendy's mother had to have emergency surgery. Then, during the operation, she had a stroke. She never recovered consciousness. For Wendy, who had to cope with losing her remaining parent as well as with an ongoing lawsuit, this was a terrible end to what she had hoped would be a rewarding new phase in her mother's life.

"I remember when I started realizing that Mom was hesitant to tell me certain things because she wasn't too sure about it herself," Wendy recalls. "We had a very tearful conversation. She told me that she had lent him money and he hadn't paid her back. She needed my help to resolve some of these issues. And I said, 'Don't worry about it. I'll help you out. Let's send him home.' Our plan was that as soon as she got through this surgery and was a little more stable with that, we would get some money together and get him out of the house, move him back to his old apartment. Then she had a stroke, and I went through all these horrible emotions. My mother was in a coma and going to die, and here's this man living in her house and he had been taking advantage of her for the last year. And I just hated him and wanted him the hell out of there. And that was another difficult issue to deal with." Wendy did follow through with her mother's legal proceedings, and ultimately reclaimed her mother's house. Her victory was bittersweet, because her mother was not there to share it. Still, she received some satisfaction from the knowledge that she had helped her mother during her final crisis, and had ultimately won her battle.

"My mom was not a stupid woman. My mom was smart. In this instance she didn't make the best decision and she regretted that and was embarrassed about it. At one point, she said, 'You know, I went out to Dad's grave and talked to him about it.' She missed him so much. She relied on him so much for making the right decisions in her life." To a great extent, Wendy realizes now, when her mother was facing great difficulty, she looked to her daughter to take over that role. At that point Wendy felt that this was the right thing to do.

For Wendy, her mother's changing needs required different levels of involvement. Although her situation ended with grief, it also came about with openness, communication, and love. Theirs was a relationship that could grow and change. Her mother's dependency, finally, was appropriate, and Wendy remembers her mother with respect.

Our Mothers, Ourselves

Coming to terms with our mothers is crucial to coming to terms with ourselves. What may be less obvious, especially in light of the complex and frustration-fraught relationships most of us report, is how much happiness we can find in these new relationships. We are meeting new women, adults with whom we already share history and bonds of love. It is no surprise, really, that the Barnett study concluded that adult daughters' reports of positive relations with their mothers were significantly correlated with their reports of healthy self-esteem and overall happiness, life satisfaction, and optimism.

The issue is one of balance, of how much importance we give to another person in our lives and how stable we are in our own autonomy. I recognize this in my own life always a day too late—a day after I've gotten furious with my mother for what I have heard as callousness to my life-or-death problems or become frustrated with hesitations that would be acceptable in any other seventy-year-old woman, but not in my mom. My goal, I tell myself, is to shorten that reaction time, to look at how I am responding as well as at her flaws—real or imagined. I am trying to reconfigure my perspective. This time, I remind myself, can be filled with discovery, not just about the women who bore us, but about ourselves, our own feelings about mothering and our own status both as children and as adults.

"Particularly for those of us who identified with our fathers, there is a pattern where you have to go get your female lineage," says psychotherapist Patricia Reis. "If you're not strong on your female ground, if you don't value yourself as a woman, and know what you are as a female, then you're in a weakened condition." Those of us who can find some connection, or at least a modicum of peace in an otherwise difficult relationship, get a more complete picture of our family history. By learning to see our mothers as women, we have an opportunity to learn more about who we are, how we grew, and who we may become.

CHAPTER 9

Work and Self-Image

Unlike generations before us, we often modeled our professional or creative lives more on those of our fathers than of our mothers. In turn, our fathers often looked to us to be the fulfillment or continuation of their professional, intellectual, or artistic selves just as they sought to protect us. These drives, often combined with a masculine ambivalence about the proper role of women in the home and in society, could produce conflicting messages for us. When these messages are no longer being given or reinforced, our feelings about our careers and projects often make a major shift. This chapter examines how our goals change, and ways in which women have implemented these changes.

My mother was an artist, but my father had a job. My mother spent her days creating images out of nothing, out of oil and air

157

and the foul-smelling chemicals that bit into the metal etching plates. She painted and made collages, ripping rice paper and daubing it with the thick paints that, globular and gelid, seemed too dense, too substantive to be paint as I knew paint through my brightly hued tempera jars and watercolor sets. And maybe it was just my later, revisionist memory that thinks of her most often at the etching press, when in truth she spent as many long hours addressing that towering easel, but when I think of the work my mother did, I imagine her at the press. Smell her, as much as see her; the oniony smell of sweat a recognizable undertone in the acrid fug of stinging acids and oily bases, of the thick, dark inks that covered the plates, and the strange solvents that cleaned them afterward. When I remember my mother's labor, the work she put herself to after she bore me, I see her turning the big handle that pulled the plates along the track, their spongy layers of paper squeezing down into the grooves and surfaces and slowly rising, just a bit, as they emerged, transformed, at the other end.

My mother was an artist, and her paintings and etchings hang on my walls now. Although she has since basically quit, given up her serious studio time for other pursuits, during her years of painting and etching she was good, no Sunday dabbler whose inexperience shows in the occasional flaw of color or awkward line. She was both talented and practiced enough so that her vision shone through, her hands served as the tools of her will and her mind. A serious artist—which to me still means unsentimental, if not unsexed—with the eye and the talent to transcend the labor of a basement studio. Her works tended toward the grim: geometrical studies of a turkey vertebrae. A portrait of her older daughter, my ill sister, as cool and posed as if of an eighteenth-century duchess. A dream image of flight, half bird and half woman and a weather-vane pointing a clean, straight path over the curves of a body at rest. Feminine preoccupations, perhaps, certainly the tools to hand were the ones of the kitchen and the nursery, unless you take exception to the darker poetry, the Dante and the Eliot, that also sparked her visual mind. But with nothing of softness. In her art, my mother may have admitted to despair, but not weakness, and what she did, she did with style. She was too good to be known, primarily, as a doctor's wife.

But if she was the one with the talent, he was the one with the job. No—a profession, a calling. For he loved the office and the hospital rounds, the chats with patients, and the routine that got him up early six days a week and kept him late on Thursday evenings. As the only son of immigrant Jewish parents, he was set on a road toward academic, and then professional success early on. Not for nothing did his grandparents bring his parents over; not for nothing did his father work in dry goods to send his two children to college. Because of his family's expectations, nothing less than a profession would do, and while one of his younger uncles had become a lawyer, my father's early bent toward science set him on the more esteemed path toward medicine. It would matter later to me, as it would for many of us, that his family and sense of responsibility had nearly nullified any consciousness of free choice he might have had, but in his case, the familial predetermination worked well. My father liked being his own boss, and he got pleasure from the slippery science that called as much on his instincts and powers of observation as on the chemistry and theory memorized at school. Plus, no matter how he denied it, he loved the role it gave him in the community, largely I suspect because he so much enjoyed spending time with people, hearing about their lives.

Not that his practice kept him from us; he made time for the family. He always came home for dinner, an almost formal affair where friends were made welcome (with notice) but never television or a book. Even if he had to retire to his study afterward to burrow into paperwork or to return calls postponed throughout the day, he would be in our house by six, seated at the head of the big rosewood table, but we knew that this was a choice, a sacrifice even, that illustrated the gravity of his position. For being a doctor also meant being respected. Later in life, he would dismiss the automatic status accorded his profession and speak disparagingly of colleagues who played god, and of the patients—particularly the older Jews and Italians who formed the bedrock of our suburb—who held their doctors in an exalted state second only to that of their rabbi or priest. But the stature fit his self-image. And if he occasionally wanted to shed it, to sit and chat with the couple from Lucca, where they made the good olive oil, or old Mrs. Butowski, the tough matriarch who still presided over three generations of hardy blond children, he could do so. Noblesse oblige. For these same motivations would have stayed him on his professional course even if he hadn't gotten a deep personal satisfaction from his work. As a family man, a good daddy in an era when traditional gender roles reigned, he believed in his responsibility to hold a steady job. Being the wage earner was part of what made him the daddy, what gave him the authority in our family home. As a result, he regarded work that provided a secure income as a necessity.

I benefited from this; all of us in the family did. As research compiled by such groups as the National Fatherhood Initiative and Dads and Daughters makes clear, an employed, respected father figure almost always results in healthier, better-educated kids. And my family certainly could have served as the perfect example. We were a solid unit, my family, at least in those early days before illness claimed my brother's life and my sister's peace of mind. My father's practice paid for horseback riding lessons for my sister, and later, the best doctors and hospitals, much as it did summer camp for me. It banished any concern I may have had about college; if I got in, which of course I would, my parents would be able to send me. In our family, higher education was expected, as much a necessity to us as milk in the refrigerator, and we came to expect it as we did the utterly unnecessary pleasantries we enjoyed, from toys to pets.

By the time I reached my twenties, I had also learned the lessons that came with this lifestyle. Hard work and responsibility pay off in security, studying and diligence will be rewarded in the kind of freedom that money can buy—freedom from want, freedom from fear. That was the first lesson, the overt one, and ingrained in me at an early age it served to keep me afloat when some of my more bohemian friends floundered in debt or faced eviction. It also gave me a sense of satisfaction that more than compensated, at first, for the succession of dull secretarial jobs that I held after college. The pleasure of paying one's own way, after all, is a liberty purchased with sweat equity. It's liberty that gender issues have made more sweet: Money of one's own is the next step up from a room of one's own, and independence is a grand, muscular joy to indulge in, akin to the pleasant hum that suffuses your body after a run.

That joy did not come undiluted, however, for the messages that were packaged underneath this clean and open moral were less welcome. For in my family, I also saw quite clearly that some people's heaviest labors were worth less than others', that the skills that I would now call qualitative, intuitive, or even feminine were less to be valued than those that could be laid out on the table, measured, and counted. The message was mixed, muddied by other theorems about responsibilities and family positions, gender and the meaning of security. But the implication, if not the text, was clear. What my father did was more important than what my mother did. What brought in the money brought in the respect, and because of their relative portions, my father was the ultimate authority in our house—about the outside world, about everything.

This was the other moral, slipped in with the joy of honest work, in my father's attitude to my mother's less profitable labors, as she left her studio to shop and cook and carpool. And this got all muddled up in his protective attitude toward me, his little girl, the one he wanted to be able to make her way in what was then (perhaps still is) a man's world. Because of this secondary set of messages I, like so many women I talk to now, inherited a mixed bag of attitudes about work and gender roles, about our freedoms to choose, and about our ability as well as our responsibility for making a living on our own. Only now, eight years after his death, am I beginning to sort out what works for me.

The Wrong Job

Was it Thursdays he worked late, or is my memory playing tricks on me? For late Thursdays, until recently, were the norm in *my* schedule: two regular days at a newspaper copy desk and one shift of ten or more hours that let me pad my weekly check, but at the cost of my temper and my nerves. Until recently, I too had a job, a claim to be a member of a profession. For nearly twenty years of my adult life I fought back the part of me that was my mother's, and like so many of my generational sisters I worked at becoming salaried, valued, paid my worth—like my father, but perhaps unlike me.

The problem wasn't the job, per se. As a copy editor at a major urban newspaper, I belonged to a union and in return for my twenty-five hours each week received excellent benefits and a decent paycheck, certainly a good wage for a single woman in these still unequal times. I spent my days there reading what I would ordinarily read for pleasure: features and reviews, stories on music and the arts. And the kinds of changes I was expected to make, the correction of a misplaced punctuation mark, the substitution of a better word to smooth out an awkward phrase, came naturally to me. I had much to learn (I have never been a confident speller) but the overall aim of the job, to aid clear communication of ideas, sat well with me.

Nor, despite the rather grimy newsroom, was the newspaper a bad place for me to be. The desks might be dusty and the air stale, but my colleagues were overall bright and witty. The crush of deadline fit my need for a bit of excitement, and the daily product, the paper that came out with our headlines, our layouts placing each story and photo just so, had its gratifying aspects. It was, and still is, the paper of record for the city. My work of each evening showed up on all my neighbors' doorsteps the next morning, and the feeling that I had participated in one step of its creation gave me a rush of satisfaction.

Of course I had my problems with the job, grumbling when deadlines occasionally made us shortchange on care and quality, and there were people in the building whom I found less pleasant than others. But somehow the time crunches and the personality clashes also made the job more real. Although my job hardly resembled the dramatic pressure-cooker atmosphere of a *Broadcast News* or *All the President's Men*, it had about it the acerbity of a proper newsroom. I could tell people where I worked and count on instant recognition. I was working at a real newspaper. I had a real job.

The problem, of course, was that it wasn't what I wanted to be doing. It was my father's idea of a career, not mine. For through the pattern of my parents' marriage, I had learned what was valued and what was not. It's a complex lesson, and one that I am still sorting out, as are countless other daughters. For despite our supposed adulthood, our supposed independence, many of us still find ourselves arranging our lives to fit our fathers' plans. "One dynamic with daughters and their fathers is they really want to please their fathers," says social worker and New York University associate professor Carol Tosone. "It means so much to them that the fathers approve of what they're doing."

This is not how we react to our mothers. It brings up what Tosone describes as "a different kind of loyalty than toward the mother, a passionate loyalty." And its roots lie, again, in our early experience of each of these parents. As with so many other aspects of our lives, we share more experiences with our mothers, and therefore we have a level of acceptance and understanding that demands less approval. With our fathers, we have nearly the same depth of connection, but we do not have the safety. How could we not, then, work for their acceptance? With fear as an incentive, how could we not rush to internalize the lessons our fathers taught?

To begin, we learned that we were expected to be able to take care of ourselves—or were we? The daughters, by and large, of working fathers and of mothers whose primary occupations revolved around raising us and keeping house, we breathed in the lesson that women's work was of less inherent value than men's. If our mothers were employed outside the house, we saw that they got paid less, got less respect, and were often told that their jobs were still secondary to their domestic duties.

Even in those families that appeared to break with tradition, the patterns held more often than not. "I thought we were beyond gender roles," says Greta, whose mother, a marketing professional, earned far more than her podiatrist father. "But looking back at our chores, the roles were there: My brother took out the trash. But I was responsible for the dishes, the kitchen, whatever needed to be done." Tally up, in her case, the additional respect accorded her father's profession, which required an advanced degree, and the financial security bought by her mother's long hours lose their importance. Her mother may have funded the long family vacations traveling across the country, but Dad did the driving.

And Greta's family was the exception. More often, if our mothers worked, they had jobs rather than careers. They earned money, rather than respect, and usually less of that than their spouses. They were, for the most part, victims of the pervasive sexism of the time, a damned-if-you-do, damned-if-you-don't set of standards that belittled them as housewives and paid them less if they ventured outdoors. The glass ceilings present today were lower then, the support of peers harder to find.

I remember coming home from school one day—I must have been in the third or fourth grade—to tell my mother of my interesting day. The teacher, I recalled, had asked us what our parents did for a living. And I had proudly told the class, during my turn, of my father the doctor. That was a real job, and one that could be easily envisioned, unlike so many of my peers' reports, which tried to explain the commute into the city or out east to the Grumman plant, to jobs that involved paper or statistics. A doctor, like a teacher or a fireman (we had no astronauts in our neighborhood), was comprehensible. We could put up the icon of a stethoscope next to my name, and we all understood what he did.

"And your mother?" I don't even remember the teacher asking me this, but I do recall reciting the event for my mother afterward. "Does she have a job?"

"No, she stays at home with me," I had said. But somehow, when I told my mother of this, my mother—who had, in fact, met me after school and was hearing me expound in the butter-yellow kitchen that was so completely our territory—was suddenly upset.

"I'm an artist," I remember her saying, her voice tense and rising. "I'm a painter. I work in my studio." Well, yes, I knew that. But a job, a real job, meant going to an office. True, her big studio was in the two lower floors of my father's office, a split-level that we had lived in until I was one year old. And when my father took over the upper floors for his practice, giving his wife the basement and half the ground floor for her papers and paints, the etching press and the looming wooden easel, he was granting her work nearly equal space with his own. And in truth, she did go there often, using the small studio in the back of our new house for smaller work, and (I now suspect) when she wanted to be available to me or my older siblings. But, although at times I found her big studio a magical cave, full of intriguing odds and ends—glass beads and bird feathers and the strange smells of turpentine and paint—it was also a dark place. These were the rooms her husband, my father, had bestowed on her once he had moved his work out—the rejects. Clearly, her work was less important than his. His world, by comparison, was full of people, of light, and of money. Plus, it took precedence over much of the ordinary, domestic, and feminine life that my mother and I shared.

That was the essential lesson that I grew up with, that so many of us who are now adults out in the world as professionals and self-supporting wage earners were nurtured on. From the beginning, we were in a bind. If we wanted respect, we would chose to emulate our fathers, not our mothers. And, at least a little, that meant accepting the values of our father's world, which granted less respect to our mothers. But I was, like my mother, a woman. Plus, as I grew up, I sought to build my life's work on the same basis of creativity, sensitivity, and intuition that had served her so well in artistic if not in financial terms. By the time I hit my thirties, I was trapped in a snare woven of gender expectations and my own dreams. It was a difficult situation, but not an uncommon one.

Emulating Father

Many women have told me of being similarly ensnared, caught between the secure "correct" path and the intuitively right one. Most often, we find the resolution in "safe" jobs, positions that pay regularly and satisfy our fathers but do not satisfy us. How could they? The norm when we were growing up was for our fathers to rule the family. And yet daughters of domineering fathers, writes Linda Schierse Leonard in *The Wounded Woman*, "often find themselves cut off from an easy relation to their own feminine instincts" and "their own creative spirit." We grow up hard on ourselves, and harder on those like ourselves, particularly our mothers. And if we follow our father's lead by divorcing ourselves from our more feminine impulses and influences, we pay for that as well. Women whose primary source of self-esteem comes from their fathers, Suzanne Fields writes in *Like Father, Like Daughter*, may find their psychological development stunted. Such a warning does not help us avoid the traps, nor undo the damage inflicted long before adulthood.

"My father told me I could do anything, and then he wanted me to be a secretary so I could have insurance," says Tracy, echoing dozens of other women who report the same mixed messages. "I'm an artist, have always supported myself in that way," adds Marcy. "But he never stopped pushing me toward teaching." Our fathers wanted us to be secure at any cost. And to be female and secure often meant accepting a lower-status position, a job that would not provoke jealousy in another, a career that involved little or no risk.

The problem reaches beyond sexism and gender roles, beyond blame. The issue lies in the conflicts that were at the heart of their feelings for us. Often, at least at first, our fathers were idealists. From our first steps, we were their talented princess-ballerina-astronauts; when we brought home our report cards we were brilliant, their very, *very* good girls. But domestic roles or support-staff positions were the norm for women in the world our fathers grew up in, and under the influence of the prevailing paradigm, perhaps our fathers' guidance in that direction is understandable. After stifling their initial idealism, our fathers probably told themselves they were realists. They undoubtedly believed that they were the ones, more often than our mothers, who saw the world at its meanest. And being our fathers, they didn't see our resiliency, our determination, or the perseverance that seeped into us at home, while they were at the office. Instead, they were grateful when we abandoned our dreams of tutus and space flight, and accepted what they considered real jobs, the kind of clerical, often menial positions they had seen women occupying since they joined the work force thirty, forty, even fifty or sixty years earlier.

Those of us who are adults today, ranging in age from our twenties to our fifties, grew up in a world different from the ones our fathers knew. As this gap makes clear, to some extent the conflict is due to our inheritance from history. We, unlike many of our mothers before us, have had unprecedented opportunities. Whether we came of age with the feminist movement, or saw our mothers, our aunts, and their friends question the roles they were raised in, we were generally the first generation of women who had such a range of choices, who overwhelmingly entered adulthood with an assumption of enfranchisement that before the 1970s belonged primarily to the very rich or the very brave. We were different from our mothers, even from our older sisters, in that we were encouraged both by these relatively new freedoms and by late-century economic realities to find our places in the markets and professions. We were not the young women our fathers had expected.

These changes were, of course, both gradual and relative. Many of our mothers and our grandmothers worked. They were pharmacists and chemists, scholars and lawyers long before graduate schools became routinely coeducational. And certainly women today, and likely still our daughters to come, will face familiar barriers, will be told that the best chefs are men, that mathematics are not feminine, and that they lack the fortitude for the military, for working in bronze, or for surgery. I do not mean to downplay these upcoming challenges or these early triumphs, but am looking instead at the larger patterns, the societal shifts that help direct our lives. For part of our problem—a contributing factor to the conflicts we face—is that, perhaps for the first time in history, we were encouraged by the outer world to be like our fathers rather than our mothers. Being an adult daughter at this time in history means, for many of us, playing out the role that a son would have in earlier generations. We are told to seize success, yet at the same time, within our families of origin, to treat these new opportunities gingerly and with mistrust, both because of their ephemeral nature and because of the conflicts between the new professional choices and our gender roles.

"The dilemma for women today is that they're expected to do both the traditional and the nontraditional," confirms Froma Walsh of the University of Chicago. We shared the socio-emotional worlds of our mothers, and yet we had a stronger identification with our fathers because our mothers, with all the constraints laid on them, "may have been disappointing as role models." Therefore the standard role of the father, to bring us into the outer world, acquired an additional weight. For those of us in the workforce today, for women from our twenties through our fifties, our fathers served dual roles, not only showing us how to relate to other people, but also, more than ever before, how to grow into our own selves.

Redirecting Misdirections

Perhaps in an ideal world these roles would complement each other. Indeed, in the work of researchers such as Esther Wachs Book, author of *Why the Best Man for the Job Is a Woman*, we learn of women whose nurturing and supportive fathers gave them a leg up in male-dominated professional fields by instilling in them a sense of goals and capability. But for many of us, these two obligations—to be dutiful, feminine daughters and also to follow our fathers professionally—came into conflict. And, once we got out on our own, the additional heft that our fathers had in our lives only served to unbalance us more. We were caught between our status as their little girls and our desire to follow in their paths. Because of our fathers' ambivalence, we learned, in many ways, to fear our freedom and to trust our insecurities more than our talents. For some of our fathers, this was a practical message and it had its roots in their history: many of them had lived through the Great Depression and had not readjusted to the realities of the contemporary economy. Add in what we have already seen of how fathers get cast in the role of protector, the guardians of their "girls" as they never have to be of sons. The conflict begins to seem inevitable.

Lori, for example, showed musical talent early. All through her student years—when her father could stand in as her protector and her caregiver—she studied her art, getting the same training as any other aspiring concert pianist. However, upon graduating, rather than pursue a performing career, she began to work as a piano technician, a tradesman of sorts that made her a kind of a handyman to the artists she had originally sought to emulate. "It's a job," she told herself as she tuned the instruments that she had been trained to play—a job that she maintained throughout her twenties, until her dad's death.

She spent a decade in this useful, but ultimately unsatisfying role. However, despite this commitment of time, she says, "I never felt totally committed to it. It was always something I was doing, kind of like being a waitress, on my way to growing up." Like so many of us who postpone following our own calling to fulfill our parents' image of success, she felt unreal, half awake. Real life was something that, without her father's support, she did not dare risk trying.

That fear dissipated, however, in the years following her father's death, and two years ago she returned to graduate school to study conducting. Although still a student, she has already secured a place with a regional orchestra—on the podium, not backstage. The change has felt natural to her, a waking up to what she really wants, as if the years spent tuning up were simply preparation for the performances she is leading now. Her one regret is that she never got to show her skill and determination to her father. "Now I look up at the sky and say, 'See? See?' It took ten years, but I'm doing it," she says.

The misdirection Lori received from her father—remember, it is from our fathers that such encouragement or direction usually comes—was not intentionally cruel. From a concerned parent's viewpoint, Lori's years as a tech made sense; she worked at a trade, instead of trusting in the vicissitudes of an art. Plus, to her father the gender barriers had seemed unsurmountable. "He would continually say, 'women can't do that. There aren't any women who are doing that.' He was very clear about it," she recalls. As an adult, the choice of whether to follow his advice or not was hers. But for Lori, as it was for me, the choice of careers was never conscious, the responsibility was abdicated before it was truly considered.

A close look at our decision-making process can help us understand how we felt about out fathers and our livelihoods. Examining career decisions may show us how we sought to please them rather than ourselves, and about how little we were able to progress without the support that they alone can give us. When we look at career choices like Lori's, we can see how we subjugated our sense of ourselves as adult women to our feelings of obligation as daughters, as well as to the fears that were more appropriate for us when we were truly little girls. We see how we made our dreams and goals secondary to those of our fathers. How we became, in the words of psychotherapist Patricia Reis, "muted women," whose personal voices were drowned out by our internalized version of our fathers'. It is their fear of the world, their overprotectiveness of us—their "hoarding" of us, as Reis explains it—that we have been reacting to, although we may have come to believe that this caution was our own inner voice. The result has been a silencing of ourselves that comes to seem almost natural, but which we sense is not truly our adult choice. The giveaway in Lori's story is in her reference to being "on her way to growing up." Those of us who let our fathers determine our professional lives postponed maturity. While our fathers were alive, we kept our real goals, our real adulthood, in abeyance to sustain the illusion that our fathers knew best.

As Lori and many of us can attest, "best" meant safest, and many of us recall years wasted at jobs that were beneath our intellectual or skill level. But high-level jobs could be safety jobs as well, and for women who longed to break free of traditional nine-to-five strictures, even a highly paid corporate job may be a remnant of someone else's dream.

Lucy, for example, had risen fairly high in a multinational corporation before her father's death. But once he passed away, she realized that her vice presidency was more what her father had wanted for her than what she wanted for herself.

"It wasn't really a cognitive choice," she says now, looking back on her days of international trading. "But, after he died, I started to get unhappy in my office time. I started to do crossword puzzles at work, and tried to avoid the morning phone calls from the UK branch. I couldn't pinpoint why, when I previously had been so driven; I had now become lackadaisical and uninterested.

"I just gradually became less and less interested in what I was doing, and one day I was in the attic at my mom's house, which had been my parents' house, and I found a book that I'd given my dad for Christmas, and on the inside I had written, 'See, Dad, if

John Updike's father made him get a corporate job, you'd have nothing to read this Christmas.' And, it wasn't until I read that, that I remembered. I'd forgotten that it was him who kept saying, 'Who's going to support you? Who's going to keep you in this life?' "

Granted, her father had practical concerns: the life of an aspiring novelist can be much harder than that of a corporate vice president. But Lucy's father hadn't counted on her innate practicality. He didn't appreciate how her business skills could be applied to build the life she would have preferred. He knew she had enough intellectual heft and determination to land an executive-level job, but he didn't trust her to know how to take care of herself. She did, and once she realized how misdirected her career had been she set about with that same diligence to get back to a more personally rewarding path. She saved, and invested wisely, and with the emotional as well as the potential financial support of her husband, she figured out how to live without the job that had begun to drain her so. Working on her first novel is hard, says Lucy, and the couple have had to learn how to budget. "Obviously now it's more a struggle," she says. "But when it's fulfilling, it's really fulfilling."

Ostensibly, Lucy's father wanted what parents are supposed to want. He wanted to see for himself that his child had become a self-sufficient adult. But rather than help Lucy find her own path, he had pushed and ridiculed her into a career that mattered more to him than to her, a career that ate up more than a decade of Lucy's adult life.

Such paternal misdirection may stem from a laudable concern. But it may also camouflage a deeper issue, a conflict that has surfaced for many women who, in the wake of their fathers' influence, are trying to figure out just what career path truly suits them. Because it is in the arena of work and career that gender issues come into play most subtly. For our fathers, this is the area where their deepest emotions about our self-sufficiency may have run up against each other in ways that have scarred our lives. For despite our new-found economic autonomy and responsibility, we are not our fathers' sons. Despite our high-level careers and stock options, we are their daughters, their little princesses, and for too many of our fathers the sight of us fighting for our rights, sweating through the long hours, and, yes, learning to rely on our strengths, was repellent. At some level, for many of our fathers, whatever work we did was secondary to our future roles as wives and mothers, and any attention we paid to career or creative success was time and energy taken from what they perceived as our proper calling. Particularly if our mothers did not work outside the house, they may have believed that a career was only a second-best fate, and we may have incorporated their prejudice that even success in our chosen field could carry the mark of our failure as women.

For Grace, who was pushed toward what she describes as a "nice, safe, feminine" career in nursing, the message was clear: unlike her mother, who did not work outside the home, Grace was not "feminine." Grace's mother was both petite and pretty. Grace has always been both tall and heavy, and early in her girlhood her father seems to have decided that she was not destined to be "successful" as a woman. Therefore, he steered her toward vocational programs, and taught her by example how he had become a success in his managerial job through diligence and determination. His lessons have served her well, but the implication remained that she would need a job to support herself because she probably wouldn't find a husband.

"I have always been heavy," she says, and corrects herself: "I *am* overweight. And I picked up this feeling that I would never get married because of this, that somehow I wasn't quite good enough."

Her father was wrong, and before he died he saw his daughter not only happily married and the mother of two sons, but also a successful medical administrator. However, the mixed definition of success that he delivered to his daughter recoils on her occasionally, despite years of therapy.

"It's very clear to me that at my work, I'm like my dad. I'm decisive. I'm clear-thinking. I can take an action immediately—

that's always been my way of operating. I can *do* things. But being so competent, I feel less than feminine. I have to remind myself that I'm good at what I do. I enjoy it. And that what matters is me as a person, not whether I'm feminine or not. But it's that old thing again: you won't be able to get married and lead the ultimate feminine role, so you'll *have* to work."

Competency was a surrogate, a means of survival for a daughter who was seen as less than a woman. That moral still makes it difficult for Grace to enjoy her professional success. "I was expected to learn to take care of myself," says Grace. "Because it was assumed that nobody would want to take care of me."

Body Image

In terms of competency, especially in the sexual arena, what our fathers thought and expressed about our bodies stays with us. These days, discussion of eating disorders tends to focus on the women who have them—on our denial of our own sexuality, and thus the fat that helps define our secondary sexual characteristics and that we can either starve away or load up on as protection. We talk about our anger, which eats at us, and thus sets us on a track of either destructive consumption or the rejection of food. But while it is good to seek understanding of our motives, important to feel we own our problems as a step toward owning our bodies, we cannot ignore the shadows lurking behind our anxieties and phobias, our obsessions and our unhealthy habits. In the morass of sexuality and body image, control and abdication of control, we must see the shadow of our fathers, of their early influence on us, on our "differentness" and our essential femininity. For if our jobs were at least partly manifestations of their control of us, then how much more must our attractiveness as women be seen as indicators of their success or failure as fathers and as men.

Among contemporary fathers, many of whom are actively battling the prevalent sexism of society, the topic is hot. Joe Kelly, the founder of the nonprofit support and advocacy group Dads and Daughters, notes that many fathers may not even be aware of the messages they are sending, particularly if they objectify other women—the girl's mother or women in the media—in her presence. He encourages fathers of daughters to focus on "what's inside, not what's outside," and to encourage physical activity and sports involvement to foster a healthy body image and to diffuse the sexual tension that often exists between fathers and young women.

"If I see one of my daughters lying by the pool in a new bathing suit, I could say, 'Is that your new suit? It looks tight, like you need to lose weight.' Or I could say, 'Is that your new suit? How is it to swim in?' " Although Kelly is trying to present the alternatives, unhealthy and healthy, for a father with an adolescent daughter, he tellingly ignores the responses that may be more common, that of reacting to the burgeoning sexuality of a daughter who is enjoying a new bikini by either becoming inappropriately flirtatious or by withdrawing completely in confusion. Both are, as Victoria Secunda points out in *Women and their Fathers*, a father's potential reactions to his own sexual attraction to this new woman. Both are hurtful, and both may injure our sense of ourselves as healthy, attractive, and sexually awakening women. The subtleties of incestuous interest wreak their own havoc, even when the transgression is never physical, as when a father inappropriately lavishes attention on a pubescent daughter and creates tension in the house. Such was the case for Barb, who can now say "I know my mother was jealous. He'd say, 'How's my beautiful girl?' And she'd point out, 'You have *two* girls!' "

The overreaction, when a father retreats in fear, can wound as well. "Once I turned fourteen, our relationship really changed," says Liza, still audibly wounded by her father's withdrawal. "I often felt he didn't accept my growing up," adds Liza. "He treated me like I was twelve years old much of the time. For years he called me on Sunday and Wednesday nights at seven, and I felt I had to be home for his calls or he'd get this accusing tone to his voice the next time we talked, and he'd say, 'You weren't home last night.' " In retrospect, she understands his difficulty. He was an old-fashioned man, a farmer and physical laborer with only an eighth grade education, and he did not know how to deal with his daughter's sexuality or his own response to it, so he ignored it as best he could. But the price Liza paid for his confusion was her self-esteem, her sense that her sexuality was wholesome and to be treasured. "And now I don't know how much my feelings about his control, his not letting me grow up, were real. We never talked about that level of things. And his feeling that I would someday move back 'home,' to my parents' home, irked me to the end."

As his two daughters traverse their teen years, Joe Kelly hopes to forge a middle way. By his example and in his work with Dads and Daughters, he is hoping to teach other fathers how to maintain their proper parental roles. Fathers, he stresses, should use their significant paternal influence on body and professional image in more egalitarian and helpful ways.

Perhaps they will manage to raise healthier daughters, women who love their bodies. Historically, however, our era has witnessed an increase in harmful overinvolvement, or inappropriate involvement by fathers. In *The Body Project*, Joan Jacobs Brumberg looks through time at how society and the family have viewed young women's bodies. She sees an increasingly unhealthy parental attitude toward control and change. "Certainly there is a modicum of parental investment that middle-class parents make in the name of hygiene and health that is absolutely normal and part of the march of progress of scientific medicine," she tells me when we talk, naming increasing paternal involvement in daughters' regular physical exams, or in orthodonture appointments and sports involvement. "Then there are other pieces of it that may in fact dip into the pathological. Is it a good thing," she asks, "for a father to jump at the opportunity to fund his daughter's plastic surgery in adolescence?" She writes about the rise in such cases, and wonders where we as a society will draw the line.

Among women who are now adults, this is a subject spoken about obliquely. One woman remembers that "Dad used to always ask me when I was going to go to the beauty parlor." She laughs, a little embarrassed by the recollection. "I think he wanted me to just be the best I could have been." Another comments on a professional colleague who regularly weighed his daughters all through their teenage years to make sure they weren't getting "too fat." The interplay of sexuality and control reeks of incest, albeit in a removed form. It feels too close for comfort, too intimate to be entirely appropriate. Plus, it brings to mind an earlier, more sexist era, with mores that are no longer our standard. The cool appraisal of our physical attractiveness, in some way our "market value," is that of a farmer preparing his livestock for auction. It may come, in part, from when our fathers looked to marry us off to ensure our security, but it now has implications far beyond paternal care. Particularly when our fathers ignored our emotional or professional growth in favor of our sexual attractiveness, this solicitude is more a burden than a blessing. In the guise of preparing us for the arena of sexual marketing, it brings those meat market's values into the home, teaching us to believe that conventional beauty translates to personal value.

Making us "pretty" as a means of making us successful may have a deeper motivation as well, one somewhat more innocuous than we may have suspected. In some way, beauty may be an achievement in the eyes of our fathers, and simply be another of the professional or domestic goals we can fulfill for them. For to be beautiful—as to be sensitive or creative—may be yet another of our fathers' failed or abandoned desires. For example, just as the son of a disappointed ballplayer may be pushed to achieve in sports, so may the daughter of a consciously machismo man be pushed into societally defined femininity—partly to fit an understood and accepted definition of worth as a woman, but partly, as well, because it may express a father's unspoken and unrealized dreams.

Perhaps the two desires are inextricably linked. "I wish I was a pretty girl," wrote the singer Robyn Hitchcock, explaining that if he were, he could have sex with himself. I remember playing this record (on vinyl, back in those days) for my parents, thinking to win them over to the British musician's quirky wordplay and lyrical melodies. I did not expect my father to notice this song in particular, but I remember that he did and that he told me he identified with it.

"That fantasy is quite common, actually," I believe he said when I looked up, silent in my surprise. The idea of being the pretty girl, "the desired object" in my father's somewhat formal phraseology, made one—made *him*—less vulnerable. In such a fantasy, one became what one wanted, he explained. Perhaps because he had allowed himself such fantasies, and come to some degree of understanding of them, my father never became overinvolved in my appearance, nor did he shy away from me as my body matured.

Years later, I would read Patricia Reis's theories on this phenomenon: "The daughter often carries things for the father," she writes in *Daughters of Saturn*, "some part of his life that is not allowed him by the culture or his own personality." For some women, that burden may include femininity, conventional prettiness, or even the kind of sexual control that men may grant women. We come to live their dreams as well as their fears.

When our fathers did not achieve their goals and have not made peace with these failures, we may become the instruments that fulfill their wishes in more conventional formats as well. This displacement rings true in the stories of women who succeeded where their fathers failed and in the tales of fathers who gave up creative goals to fulfill societal or familial ones.

Lori's father, for example, might have had some deeper conflicts about her desire to find a career in the arts; he had been a disappointed architect. Between his army duties and the necessity of earning enough to support his family of four, he had given up plans for graduate school and accepted a civil service post. The job had its advantages, but Lori learned of his long-delayed dreams upon his retirement, when he once again picked up pen and paper. He became an accomplished amateur artist in his later years, throwing himself once more into the world of the imagination. The difference, his daughter explains, was that the rubric of retirement allowed him to return to his dismissed dream without dealing with the reality of his professional disappointment. His art, by then, was a hobby instead of a path not taken, and thus carried less weight. "He was doing it to amuse himself. It wasn't serious," she explains.

I see some similarities in my own family story, and place my father among the men who abandoned risky artistic endeavors to become steady breadwinners. For whether or not my father was plagued by his failure to be an object of beauty and desire, I do believe he did feel his creativity had been stifled.

The early clues were small, and easily missed. He would complain about the direction medicine was taking, repeat with disgust stories of medical schools' increasing reliance on tests and chemistry, and of the lagging wisdom of his younger colleagues. Small stuff, really. The kind of complaints many feel in a changing world. I didn't realize that he saw himself as a creative person until early in his retirement, when he informed me that he was engaged in writing a history of his shortwave radio club—that, as the historian for the club, he was researching and preparing to write a magazine article about the first wireless club in this country, if not the world.

I wished him luck, and thought little about it until I saw how his project was growing to consume him. With a mix of trepidation and sympathy, I heard about him bullying librarians for materials, assuming his old doctorly status automatically when he sought help from someone he deemed a clerical type. Gingerly, I tried suggesting a word limit—or at least a query letter—to the alumni magazine he had in mind. He ignored me, hearing my offers of experience as only an eager reader's curiosity, and the pages accumulated.

At that time, I had spent more than a decade learning the rules of the profession that he was assuming a knowledge of, and I had also written many articles for the magazine he intended as the publisher of his opus. Like him, I was attached to the alumni magazine by college affiliation, but I was also a professional journalist. Looking back, I must have resented this intrusion into my territory, this presumption of knowledge with its implied dismissal of all my years of work, but I remember no anger or feeling of violation. All I knew then was that I was worried about him, fearing the moment that I suspected would come, when the magazine would reject his opus for being too long and unfocused.

When it happened, it happened gently. In respect for an alumnus and as a courtesy to me, I suspect, the editor did tell my father that he would be happy to read a revised version, provided my father cut his manuscript down to magazine length and perhaps find one relevant event to tie it to. His advice as to how to do such revisions was generous, more than most busy editors would give to first-time aspirants. I thought my father had been set on the right path. But rewriting, the real work of writing, would never happen: a wealthy member of the club paid for a handsome edition of my father's work to be published as a small book, with a Harvard crimson binding and my father's name on the cover in gold.

His publishing, his desire to author a book and, by extension, to succeed in my chosen field, was out of my control. I did not let him publish anymore than he allowed me to write. But I did choose to bite my tongue as he ventured into my field, and I do not know if I did so more out of love or fear or pity. I never acted as if we were rivals. Although he would ramble on a bit about his research and the interviews he was compiling, I never pointed out that such a vanity publication would not stand up in literary terms to the work I was doing and had already done, and by my silence I let him have the upper hand in our unstated competition. By the time the book arrived from the printer, he was ill. How could I take his triumph away from him? The better question may have been, how much did I deflate myself to remain smaller, lower, and more the subservient girl child? At the time I told myself that my silence did not cost me much, but it was a degradation of my field, a way of devaluing my work, and I suspect that I absorbed the cost as I had much else over the years—one more body blow to my independence and to the confidence I had been trying to build in my work.

Not all of us kept our heads bowed. At times, perhaps particularly if we were motivated as their surrogates, we reacted by throwing our success into their faces. We were as tough as they were, we earned as much money as they did, if not more. But in doing so, we often swallowed our ambivalence about this competitiveness, and found ourselves as unbalanced by our success as we might have been by failure.

"My father never felt like a success," says Raquel. Her father, a North African immigrant, was the vice president of a major advertising firm when he died of bone cancer, but despite his success in his adopted country, she explains, he never believed that he had made it on his own merits. "He felt like a token hire," she says, "He never felt the value of his work."

For Raquel's father, several elements come into play, notably the racism that he found when he first came to this country. To an outside observer, he seemed to regard the barriers set up by society as so many hurdles just waiting to be jumped. Inside the family, however, Raquel saw a man who was bewildered and almost broken by a system he didn't comprehend. It was a system that his daughter, now a vice president in advertising herself, would conquer.

"I think for a really long time I just strove to be successful," she says. "That was my dad's voice driving me because I felt like that's what he really wanted for me." It was what he wanted for himself as well, and because he never felt secure in his achievements, the constant "striving for success and acceptance," as she remembers it, was passed along. Raquel has benefited from it, inheriting her father's tenacity as well as his will to succeed. This past year, she was one of only twenty employees at her firm to survive a hostile takeover, and one of only three management-level employees to do so. Because she succeeded, she says, she mystified her father. "I think my father was afraid of me," says Raquel. "I was the only one of us he was afraid of."

Still, the drive she inherited is not entirely organic for Raquel, and the discrepancy between what she could do and who she wanted to be finally became apparent in the years following her father's death. It's been hard, especially because she is good at what she does, but these days she's trying to expend some of her massive energy in more personally satisfying ways.

"I have found that I really need to balance my life more," she says. "I see my friends; I read pathologically," she says laughing. "I go to movies now." Recently, she's also found herself returning to music. She's taking guitar lessons again, as she did as a teenager, and as she picks out the chords slowly she talks about her father's love of music, of opera in particular. It's definitely a point of connection with the confused and often bitter man she mourns. But it's the job, not the art, that she still feels he would recognize.

"Sometimes I wish that he was still around so he could see how far I've come," she says, wistfully. "I make the same amount of money at thirty-six that he made when he died."

True Expectations

Only when we lose our fathers, when the active elements of their fears and hopes and their own frustrated dreams are removed from our lives, do we see how all these issues of work and value play out. If our fathers were, ideally, our first and strongest connection with the outside world, we may experience a tremendous loss of support when we lose them, more so than if we lost our mothers. But when the support was undermined by inappropriate expectations or inaccurate fears, then when our fathers are taken from us, we are also freed from this particular pressure. We are free, finally, to explore our own expectations.

For some of us, that means a return to the more practical, remunerative careers that we fled after too many years of our father's urging. "Once he'd died, I realized I'd wasted a lot of energy fighting what he wanted for me," says Marcy, who has come to enjoy teaching as an adjunct to her painting. "And what he wanted were good things."

For others, our initial reaction may be one of relief. At a father's death, explains Carol Tosone, a woman may experience a new sense of freedom. "There's nobody looking over your shoulder anymore," the social worker explains. The result can be a tremendous release of energy, a sudden clarity of purpose. "Once my father died," remembers Greta, she experienced "a redefinition of self and a reorientation of goals.

"I suddenly felt like—holy shit!—if I want to do good in my life, if I want to achieve things, I have to do it! *I* have to do it." After years of playing guitar in garage bands, supporting herself through temporary jobs, she applied to law school.

"I became goal-oriented in ways I'd never been before," agrees Linda, a commercial artist with a design portfolio that now boasts full-color spreads from several national magazines. Although her talent is apparent in the glossy layouts, her mathematician father had never understood or supported her career. Instead, he was prone to screaming rages, during which he'd insult her supposed lack of intellect and drive. As a result, Linda says, "I was so afraid of making the wrong choice that I'd make *no* choice." All that began changing after her father's sudden death from a heart attack, brought about in part because of his heavy smoking and drinking. His death, when Linda was twenty-nine, freed her to pursue her art without the fear that he was looking over her shoulder disapprovingly, and in the ensuing decade she has blossomed. Almost immediately after his death, she says, "I began seeking out professional and creative challenges."

Without a history of paternal encouragement, Linda reports that her road toward success has been rocky. "My feelings about my creative abilities still flounder," she says. "But I began to do, and pursue. I became proactive as never before."

As these women demonstrate, our choice of career is not the issue. While Lori went from a trade into music, Greta swung from music to the law, and Linda found herself free to wholeheartedly pursue the commercial arts and graphics that had always interested her. What we see in these women, instead, is the shift in confidence, a shift in focus to our needs and to our own dreams.

Our fathers may have built us up to believe in ourselves, but too often while they were part of our lives they also held us back. At times they seemed to have a vested interest in keeping us dependent as they sought to make us into ideal women or to assuage their own sense of failure. And at times we were too caught up in rebelling to recognize what we were capable of, too angry to settle back and realize that we all wanted the same good things for our futures. More often than not the waters were so muddied that all these factors came into play.

I don't think it is any accident, nor should it be a huge surprise, that one of the first pieces I wrote in my new, more free style was about my father, as is this book—my exploration into the convoluted father-daughter relationship. My father taught me by example about work, about the pleasure of a hard-earned victory. And if I inhaled his fear along with a sense of entitlement, his hesitation along with his pride, at least now I can begin to discriminate between these parts of his legacy. Like so many aspects of my relationship with my father, I can now lay them out like seashells on the table before me, to sort and admire, and sometimes to discard, before putting them away in my memory box and getting back to work.

CHAPTER 10

When Lives
Do Not Change

The changes covered in the preceding chapters are pervasive trends. However, for many women, the father's death does not immediately or necessarily lead to marriage or divorce or a change in employment. This chapter looks at the women whose relationships with others and with their jobs do not shift in the light of their relationships with their fathers. For although these women appear to share a certain stability, there may actually be several factors at work. Some women, for example, seem unable to change unhappy or destructive familial patterns even once they have lost their fathers. The damage has been too deep. And, conversely, some women have had such happy and natural relations with their fathers that the loss, while grieved, does not disrupt the patterns of their lives. In some ways, this chapter focuses on the women who have had the most extreme relationships with their fathers.

Sometimes it's the smallest things—the kitchen timer that needs to be replaced or the forgotten milk from the shopping list—that jar us back to life. Alarm clocks ring and—once we've started sleeping well again—we begin again to curse them and ready ourselves for work. The cat, if all cats are like mine, coughs up a furball on the rug again and stares as reproachfully as always, waiting for someone else to clean up the mess. And we do. Willing or not, we respond to these mundanities as we emerge from grief, and it's these small details that supply the proof that life is, after all, continuing.

The triviality of all these continuing minor duties often strikes us as disrespectful. How dare our lives continue, we may think, when our fathers have died? But even if we believe our entire world should look different, that all the colors of autumn should be cloaked in gray, the world is not usually compliant. Time itself betrays us by its obstinacy. Despite our loss it continues, carrying with it the day-to-day duties of jobs and laundry and chores that comprised the bulk of our waking hours when our fathers were alive and which seek once more to fill our days. Bills pile up and need to be paid and, as the days and weeks and months pass, routines that had been broken are reassembled.

For me, the daily duties that picked up after my father's death were different only in that they had become more solid, and more mundane. I had been a temporary worker at the newspaper when he died, and a few months later the next temporary position I was occupying opened up as a permanent job. After working there more or less full time for several years, I was finally an actual staff member of the newspaper. I recognized this as success after a fashion; my years of diligent labor in various copy editing positions had finally been rewarded with job security and health insurance. And because there had been a few tense weeks while some other editors tried out for the job, I did enjoy the pleasant flush of triumph when I got the call offering me the position that, in fact, I had already occupied for several months. The desk was mine now, and soon I brought in a photo of my new boyfriend, Jon, to personalize its steel surface, to claim it as my own.

But the job, although stable and well paying, was far from the type of position I had dreamed about, and the security it offered was in several ways a retreat from the progress I'd been making over the past few months. By the time I was made a member of the staff, I was writing regularly and well; both I and the editors who were publishing my stories recognized that these articles were stronger, clearer, and cleaner than any of my previous work. I'd begun to think of turning one of my magazine pieces into a book. Readers were beginning to recognize my name, and colleagues to encourage me to take myself seriously as a writer. But that's not what the job I had landed asked of me. The job I had just won was much like the ones I had filled for years: a copy editing position that had me reading and correcting other writers' stories, looking for errors in grammar and punctuation, and basically serving as the last line of defense before publication. It was a job that called for skills I had, but was best suited for a different kind of temperament, a more careful, detail-oriented type of creativity. It was an honorable job, and a good career for many. But I had never thought of myself as primarily careful; I had never given a priority to rules or to grammar. Yet I accepted the job, and there I stayed.

My reasons, at first, were obvious, even to me. My father had died, I needed a respite from turmoil. I'd had enough, for a while, of upheaval, and the paper had come to feel familiar. Plus, my blossoming romance with Jon served as a distraction, providing enough excitement to make the long hours correcting others' mistakes at a poorly lit computer terminal tolerable.

I am also tempted to add that the financial security was appealing. But although the weekly paycheck was nice, it didn't have the same weight for me that it did for my colleagues who were parents or who had mortgages to meet. I didn't need much. Plus, the recent success of my writing had shown me that my work had value in a monetary sense as well as an artistic one. Ever since I had found myself limited by my own lack of savings, I'd made a habit of watching my accounts and paying bills promptly just so I would never be trapped in a dead-end job again. But here I was opting for a position I didn't want. With these thoughts brewing in the back of my mind, the new job was a bit of a letdown, as if it underlined my father's dictate of years before. I was being safe, I was choosing regular work over my very real—and not utterly unrealistic—career aspirations. I was agreeing with the world that my dreams of making a living with my writing were not going to be realized.

As I've said, I understand why I took the job. It was a good offer, and it was probably a sound move at the time. A healing, calming, exceedingly regular place to be. But later, when I realized that I was approaching my seventh year there, having already published one book and numerous magazine articles, I had to doubt my motives. The dream was still there, and the job still as far from it as I could imagine while remaining in the same field. My father's death had freed me from so many forms of internalized repression that I had found my way to love and a satisfying marriage. My art reflected this late-blooming freedom. And yet somehow, when it came to this job, there I was, resolutely stuck.

A Healthy Stability

Clearly, not everyone's life gets turned around by crisis. Among all the women I've spoken to for this project, there have been many whose lives did not change, who went through no dramatic rebirth or enlightening self-discovery after their fathers' deaths. These are the women who have already integrated the pluses and minuses of childhood into their lives as adults, who have made peace with their parents and moved on. I tend to think that these people are in the minority, and they are certainly less well represented in this book. Because they are less involved with my topic, less interested in how their loss changed them, these women tended to be the least willing to be interviewed. However, the ones who did consent to talk to me usually find, after a half hour of chat that yes—surprisingly—it was about a year or so after their fathers' deaths that they decided to go back to school, quit drinking, have a second child, or open that small gallery.

I always made a point of leaving my questions open-ended, but just bringing women back to the months immediately following the deaths of their fathers almost invariably turned up some change, some shift, that they hadn't before connected to their loss. Sometimes their original reasoning seemed sound, and the events were not related. More often, once they started talking, they were the ones to draw the connections, to realize that the new program reflected something about the man who died, or about the way he had tried to direct them in the world.

It may make sense at this juncture to reiterate that recognizing the impact of our fathers on our lives does not simply involve placing blame. Some of our fathers did their jobs well. They listened when we spoke and were curious about our lives. Some were as benevolently involved as possible, playing out their parts as guides and then freeing us to explore the outside world. Some, perhaps more often than we want to admit, were simply the best parents they could be under the circumstances. Even when we feel their influence was misused, with time we may come to understand the pressures they were under, and to forgive them for being less than we needed. Even those of us who in later years have found their influence toxic may recognize that some of what our fathers shared with us was good. And in such cases, the changes we note after their deaths may be minor. We grieve, certainly, but we have already grown up. We miss them from our lives, but we were already launched as adults and no longer needed them as we did when we were children. In such cases as these, the alterations we find when they are gone from our lives are those that come from sadness and from intimate knowledge of death. The disruption is part of our grief. We may be unbalanced, but that unease tends to be temporary. We may experience the elation that comes from the realization of life's preciousness. We may find ourselves with a growing awareness of life's—or our own—spiritual nature. What we come back to, ultimately, is a deeper appreciation for the solid foundation these good fathers gave us.

Bette's life serves as an example of such steadiness, a sense of security and self-assuredness that comes at least in part from the love and support her father gave her. Happily married for twenty-three years, secure in her career as a public-interest lawyer, Bette has learned to rely on her own internal steadiness and sense of worth to help her cope with several losses, including those of her four-year-old niece and younger sister.

Not that such tragedies have been easy. In fact, when Bette lost her father six years ago, she found herself additionally hurt by the callousness of family members, in particular the oldest of her three brothers. In a pattern that may be familiar to other women with siblings, this brother seemed to naturally assume their father's position. But the decisions he made about the family business—decisions that adversely affected their widowed mother—were not the ones their father would have made. Plus, Bette says, when she tried to talk to him, to explain what she saw as errors or discrepancies, her brother refused to discuss the business with her.

"Larry seemed to be turning into a monster," she said. "And I was so hurt, I was furious with him." With time, she came to see that her brother's selfishness was not a new development, that Larry had always been "on his own track," as Bette puts it. His flaws were simply more visible now. What Bette had to do was accept that her brother was the same rather selfish person that she had known from childhood. And that the lessons she had learned—to put her trust and affection in her husband rather than in the eldest of her brothers—were still valid, despite her brother's assumption of their father's role.

"I really was looking for someone to take my dad's place and be this nice caring person in my hometown," she acknowledges. "When I realized I was doing that, I asked myself: What do I need my oldest brother to step into my father's place for? I have a perfectly happy marriage and a husband who is not childish. He is a grown-up. I realized that my husband was always there and that if I was looking for somebody who would always approve and always love me and always be there, even with absurd requests, I already have that in my husband Frank. So I sort of settled down and relaxed and stopped trying to find my dad."

Bette's family is real, not ideal, and because she misses her father very much she was vulnerable. Despite her usual stability, she opened herself up to a hurtful experience with her brother in a way that many of us will recognize. Because of her longing for her father, she let her brother usurp his place. In the words of family therapist Terry Hargrave, "A natural process of grief is that people have to emotionally relocate the person who is lost." In Bette's case, she temporarily "misplaced" feelings of loss and dependence onto her brother. "Then, you come to grips with their influence on your life," Hargrave says. True enough, because Bette had other strong and loving relationships—with her other brothers and her mother as well as with her husband—she was able to regain her equilibrium and withdraw from a painful situation.

Although many factors certainly play into her life, Bette credits the warm relationship she had with her father for much of the love she has now gathered around her. Although their relationship had flaws, it left her with a strong sense of her own worth, which allowed her to find security as an adult long before he died and left her.

"I was special to him," she says now. "I was his beautiful girl." Comfortable in his pride and love, she was able to find both for herself as an adult. For Bette, as for many of the best-adjusted women with whom I spoke, change was the aberration. As her grief eased, she was able to relax back into the security of her former life.

Frozen in Time

For others of us, however, the lack of change may feel more like an inability to grow. Frozen by unresolved grief or by conflicts that we never had the chance to fight through, we may find ourselves deadlocked in our careers or creative ventures. We may be unable to resolve romantic or familial relationship issues, stuck repeating unhealthy patterns that first became apparent years before. We may find ourselves regressing, stepping back into the kind of unhappy situations we thought we had outgrown.

Certainly, some of this sterility is fed by outside factors: the ongoing influence of the other people in our lives—friends or siblings or mothers. And some of our problems are secondary, manifestations of deeper troubles or addictions we've developed that undercut our efforts to succeed and change. But sometimes, most clearly in the areas that we associate with our fathers' influence, we are simply stuck. Whether we felt we loved our fathers or we hated them, we don't know what to do without them; we don't know how to function without their direction. For women like Perri, who had defined herself in opposition to her stern father, the sudden absence of the need for defiance is perhaps the most confusing aspect of all.

"I've always been the type of person who didn't need to have any reinforcement from anybody else about the decisions I was making," she says. "My dad was always giving me feedback, usually unwanted feedback. I had always rebelled against listening to what he was saying. And then I didn't have anything to push against anymore and it was really hard. It was hard to make that change because then I knew I was on my own and I was making my decisions."

Perri tried to engage her mother in the same kinds of arguments that she formerly had with her father, but her mother was of a more pacific temperament. She believed her daughter, at twenty-six, was old enough to make her own decisions. And Perri, who had grown accustomed to wrangling with her father, felt cast adrift. She realizes now that their arguments served to solidify her choices, even if she made them simply to oppose her father. Now she finds it hard to progress; she feels aimless without him. "I wanted to get some of that reinforcement after he died. I didn't realize how much I needed that in order to put myself on the straight path."

For those of us who sought to please our fathers, the inability to move forward may be more insidious. We incorporate what we remember, and react as we believe we should have, even though we can no longer accurately perceive what they may or may not have wished for us. In some ways, this can be a more difficult pattern to break from, simply because we cannot have it out with our fathers. We can no longer argue our case or hope for change. In death, they are frozen in our memories, and thus our reactions, guided by them, are not allowed to change either. Their influence, magnified by death, becomes so great that it may be years before we dare move, years before we can begin to creep out of their shadows and seek the warmth and happiness that serves as the equivalent of light.

Psychotherapist Patricia Reis talks about this unhappy repetition as one of the lingering aftereffects of a difficult father-daughter relationship. She sees it as our attempt to externalize the unresolved issues that remain after our fathers die. By re-creating the unhealthy situation in other areas of our life, whether that be in romance or work, she explains, we seek to come to a happier conclusion than we ever could with our fathers during their lifetimes. We hope to heal ourselves with this compulsive repetition of unhappy behaviors. More often we succeed in continuing to hurt ourselves.

In *The Wounded Woman*, Linda Schierse Leonard discusses the necessity of forgiving our fathers as a step toward healing the damage they may have inflicted on us through malice or ignorance. When our fathers are no longer alive, no longer available for an actual reconciliation, then the peacemaking must take place within ourselves, she says. In such cases, we must find a way to forgive our father and also to forgive ourselves for continuing these unhealthy patterns. Only then can we resolve our issues, our old anger and deep sadness, and not be ruled by them. Only then can we put away the behaviors that we have outgrown and move on.

"I remember my sister saying to me, 'Dad would hate what you've become. He'd hate the kind of feminist you've become,' " says Susan, thinking back on the changes she went through after her father died. "At first, I thought, she was right. But then I tried to work through what he would have thought if he had been around during the past few years. And I think he would have understood why I reached my conclusions." By making this kind of assumption of growth, by imagining how her father would still have loved her despite the changes in her politics, Susan made her own passages easier. "He left me with a living faith, actually, that authorizes such transgressions, if that's what they are. In short, I am still conscious, twenty years later, of the liberating coordinates of his love. He would have grown to understand what I am doing now," she says.

It's difficult to make this kind of leap. Especially if we had trouble winning our fathers' acceptance at other growth stages of our lives, it may be hard to imagine this kind of approval now. Instead, we may find ourselves trapped and clinging to a static image of what our fathers would have wanted. Unable to let go of our disappointment over not resolving our conflicts, we hold too tightly to what we imagined our fathers were, what we thought they wanted—ideals that may be as outdated as our childhood clothes.

Liza, for example, is not happy. She has not yet returned to writing songs since her father's death four years ago, and she no longer performs in the coffeehouses she had regularly graced in the years before. She is, she knows, depressed, and although she cannot tell which is the symptom and which is the cause, our conversation keeps coming back to the live-in relationship she had begun with Peter only a few months before her father's death.

Part of the problem, Liza recognizes, is that her father adored Peter and wholeheartedly approved of their relationship when she took him home to meet her family. Her father had never really given an enthusiastic thumbs-up to any of her beaus before, she explains. "I took Peter home for my parent's fiftieth anniversary and Dad fell in love with him," she says. "Peter owns his own business, which he works very hard at, and my father related to that. Plus, he's a descendent of Thomas Jefferson, and Dad loved American history. When I moved in with Peter, Dad seemed more relieved than anything. My younger sisters were both married, and I think he could finally breathe easily that I, too, had someone."

Up until this point, Liza acknowledges, this sounds like a happy story. She finds love and her rather overprotective and critical father can die content, believing his daughter is being cared for. However, this idyllic beginning failed to progress into the kind of relationship Liza wanted. Part of the problem, she admits, came about because of Peter's fear of death. He reacted badly to her father's decline into illness only a few months after they had moved in together, becoming cold and distant during her frequent hospital visits and ultimately refusing to fly back to her Midwestern birthplace for the funeral. "I don't think I'll ever forget the intense feeling of betrayal and abandonment on that snowy January night when he wasn't even with me while I was going through the actual death," says Liza.

Still, they stayed together, although Liza can't really tell if they ever completely recovered from that crisis. It's a subject they talk about a lot, and they have been going to couples therapy regularly to help work out their differences in matters of loyalty and commitment. Sometimes, Liza admits, it seems that she stays with Peter more out of loyalty to her father than because she really hopes their situation will improve. Her father had a difficult time accepting Liza as a grown woman; he hardly talked to her at all during her adolescence. And now she wants to cling to the image of adulthood that her father had accepted, the one adult relationship of which he had approved.

"His goal that I have a solid relationship and a real house and a 'forever' man, I think, is my prime motivator in sticking with this relationship," she says now, describing her father's hopes and dreams for her. "I think of how he would react if he knew some of the things Peter has said and done to me. He would be so disgusted. On the other hand, he liked Peter, and he'd be very, very sad." Because her father never lived to see how her affair had soured, she finds it difficult to accept the truth herself.

"I think of being on my own again, of being alone and single," she says. "Dad would have hated to see me like that. He would have hated for me to give up a 'good thing' like I have with Peter for that kind of insecurity." Although it is clear to both of us that Liza is making her own choices, her feelings for her father—and what he wanted—hold such weight that they have become part of his legacy for her. Although she was able to end and begin relationships while he was alive, now that he is dead she finds herself stuck in the one that he liked best, living out his dream whether it fits her life or not.

For some of us, stasis is necessary, even when the first stages of mourning have passed. I have discussed earlier how grief names its own seasons, and this is true for all kinds of healing. For those of us who have been deeply wounded, years may be necessary before we can begin to begin again.

Gigi, for example, has led a tumultuous life. Twice divorced and the mother of preteen and teenage boys, she moved back to her parents' house after her second marriage failed. Out of work and exhausted, she built her strength back up slowly. Although she found a new job and a new career (counseling other women in life transitions), she stayed at home with her parents, and helped nurse her father through the final stages of colon cancer. Three years later, she is still living in the house that she now shares with her mother. She is still single and not seeing anyone. For now—and for the foreseeable future—that is a good way to be.

"My mother's got a boyfriend, but I don't," she notes with a wry chuckle. "I'm very conscious of that. There are some times when I feel lonely, but I've got my guard up and there are a number of reasons for that. I feel very content right now. I have a roof over my head with my children and my dog. We are all happy. We are all doing well and it's kind of a nice flow. And I think a lot about who it would be that could possibly fit into that, who I would want to have there, who my children would want to have there. And I feel like right now it's time for our unit of three to just go forward. I'm very conscious of the fact that my oldest is in grade ten and he's only going to be home, really, for a couple more years; that my youngest is in grade seven, and I'm almost feeling those years slipping away. I'm almost feeling like, once they are in college, maybe then it would be time for me."

She understands, as well, how she has maneuvered herself into her current situation. "I have a really demanding job, and in the evening I work on the kids' activities," she says. "It doesn't leave a lot of time. I live in the suburbs and that doesn't lend itself a lot to meeting eligible men; I work in a women's health center, so it doesn't happen there so much, either. I'm honestly really content about that, content to understand that there are probably issues I still need to work through, that I'm still a little scared. But, at the same time, I just don't want my boat rocked right now. And I don't want my kids' boat rocked."

The key, for many of us who do feel stuck, may be to acknowledge that some changes simply take their own time. Some growth can't be rushed. But if we are careful and diligent, we can chart the little steps we are taking. We can see the progress we are making, in small and quiet ways.

"Before my father's death, I had been involved with an alcoholic, a drug addict, and a suicide survivor," says Linda. Single and lonely at forty-two, she knows that her conflicted lifelong relationship with her brilliant alcoholic father has left its mark on the romances she finds herself in. "After his death I chose quieter, more passive men," she explains. Because her parents were divorced when she was only eight, Linda falls into a category that researchers have long predicted will have relationship problems. William Appleton, for example, labeled the daughters of divorce as uniformly "distrustful" and discussed their difficulties finding an appropriate balance between intimacy and distance in their relationships with men. In *Father Loss*, Elyce Wakerman writes, "The daughter of a deceased father knows she has little choice but to cope with the acrid taste left in her mouth; the daughter of divorced parents keeps hoping the prescription will change." As a daughter who has lost her father twice, Linda acknowledges these issues. But in acknowledging them, she has taken the first steps toward healing, and she remains hopeful that with time, thought, and therapy she can change her destructive patterns. "After twelve years, I'm still trying to figure out this relationship thing, still trying to get it right," she says. "That is, my relationship with men and with myself."

As the years accumulate, Raquel also can chart her healing. Although she remains single—and on the lookout for love—she believes that ever so slowly she is unlearning the patterns of violence that her parent's abusive relationship taught her.

"I think just the fact that I'm thirty-six years old and I haven't had a successful relationship yet is indicative of the scars he's left," she says, thinking back on the father who died ten years before. "But I also think every choice I've made has gotten a little bit better. I'm aware of the mistakes, so I try not to make them again. I feel like I'm starting to run out of them. Up until a couple of years ago, I was still drawn to men who needed to take control, fighting them. This last time, I finally let myself fall in love. I let myself be taken care of, and I realize that's something I want from a man." Raquel's most recent romance still revolved around issues of safety and control, she acknowledges. But this time, she had the control. Her executive position gave her money and privileges that contrasted with her boyfriend's job as a bartender, and these external issues reflected the differences in their personalities. But although he was much more passive than she is, they did share great affection and, for a while, a love that was safe and healing for Raquel. Although they split with some tears six months ago, this is one relationship she doesn't regret.

"I've kind of made a decision this year that if my next relationship fails, I'll be okay with that. I just don't want it to fail for all the reasons that the other ones have. I don't want to make the same mistakes again," she says.

That's a worthy goal for any of us, and one that I can recognize. My issues were more with work than love, but the feeling of being stuck, of repeating mistakes because of old fears was much the same. I had to do some hard thinking about my dreams and about my fears when I neared the seventh anniversary of my job as a copy editor, and so began to compile a mental list: I had savings, I had marketable skills, I had offers of more writing work than I could accept with my editing hours. I also had—and this is a distinct advantage that not all my colleagues share—a loving and supportive husband who was willing to take on more of the household financial burden if I needed him to. I had no children or other dependents to support, nor any outstanding debt. I had, in fact, no reason to stay except the ingrained notion that it was a good job, a *safe* job, and that my father had been so happy when I had first landed at the newspaper. Then it dawned on me—slowly and accompanied by many fresh floods of fear—that hanging onto the job that had made him so proud was not a healthy way to memorialize him. That maybe he would be proud of me now for leaving, for following my dream. And if I could allow myself to believe that he would want this for me, that he would encourage me to act from my heart, then I could resurrect some of my first memories of him—my best memories, in which he was supportive of my achievements and involved with my interests. I was doing neither of us any service by remaining. And so, as 1999 wound to a close, I gave notice on the job I had held for seven years. Within a month, I had contracts to write two books and more freelance work than I could handle. I believe my father would have been proud.

CHAPTER 11

The Journey
Over Time

M any of the changes discussed in this book are sudden, happening within a year or two of a father's death. This chapter will look at the long view—at how our lives, goals, and relationships have grown and changed over time.

Time Lapse

"I'm feeling a bit peckish," my husband says to me, late on a Sunday afternoon as we sit reading and listening to music. "Would you like a little snack?" He looks at me fondly, hoping to entice me into the moderate sin of cheese and crackers, or perhaps a shared biscotti, and for a moment I am lost. That could have been my father saying those words; this could have been my parents' house, with the opera providing the soundtrack for this relaxed, sedentary afternoon. I look at my husband and remember suddenly the sweetness that I would often see in my father's face, the joy he took in small pleasures, and for a moment I am taken back. I am my father's daughter.

Then time rushes forward to the present, and I realize what I have done, how I have re-created the small rituals of my childhood here with my husband, such as sharing with him my father's pet passions—the British "peckish" for hungry, the sense that he and not my mother was the lord of treats—and another phase of growth becomes apparent.

"We incorporate elements of people we love," one wise woman said to me. "That's how we keep them alive." The phrases, the habits—all these I realize are part of my inheritance, the flip side of the fear and the self-doubt. The taste for these pleasures, in other words, as well as the guilt that for long years kept me alone and joyless. They're all one.

When I think of the changes that we all have gone through since losing our fathers, I find myself seeing the girls we were as well as the women we are now. I think of how we've grown, how we've learned to assert essential parts of ourselves that for so many reasons could not come to the fore while our fathers were alive. I also realize—as we must if we are being honest with ourselves—that so much of this growth is simply the gift of time. Nearing forty, I should be more self-confident than I was at thirty, or what has the past decade been about? Just as at forty-one Lita knows better what she wants to do than she did at thirty, and as Rona, now in her mid-forties, is better able to relax into a relationship with a good and loving partner than she could five or ten years ago. We have had time to grow into ourselves, had experiences that we have learned from, and have new people bringing joy into our lives to counter our loss and sorrow. And as noted before, many factors play into this, our present, and it would be hugely unfair to attribute all our changes to the absence of our fathers.

Better perhaps to see this one traumatic loss as the breaking of a mold, as the opportunity to recognize that the man who first held us did in fact shape us. And now that the mold of his strong influence is removed we can see what we learned from him, and where our native structure, our basic form, reasserts itself.

We need time, after all, to be able to judge which of the changes we made in response to our fathers' deaths were made in grief and which were true growth. Which, in other words, were simply reactions to his absence and which were assertions of our true selves. For some of us, the changes we went through were not meant to last. They were necessary transitions, and may have served a vital purpose—allowing us a time out to reevaluate who we were and what we honestly wanted. Rikki, for example, reconciled with her husband and had a fourth child after their initial split. The time away from him, she says now, gave her perspective and the opportunity to "put their marriage on a different footing." After that break, however, she chose to remain in the relationship. And many of her colleagues, the women in this book, report similar relationship blips—temporary, but necessary.

In her book *Daughters of Saturn*, Patricia Reis discusses such breaks in routine. After a crisis, such as a death, has freed us to reevaluate our lives, she says, we often find ourselves in what she calls the "wildzone," a state in which we feel free to experience all our previously repressed emotions, such as rage. This is when we may do most of our experimenting with relationships or with careers. It is, according to Reis, a time in which we may focus on being female, on the most female parts of ourselves, and on our relationships with other women, including our mothers.

But if we toss all our conventions to the ground, after a time we may choose to pick some of them up again. This is not failure; our time away from our usual selves has allowed us to explore options that perhaps we had not previously felt free to consider. When we return, we will no longer follow a certain career path or remain in a marriage because father knows best. But we also no longer feel a need to flee something that has worked for us simply because father had directed us toward it. After such a break, we are better able to make our own decisions, and to evaluate the influences that have acted upon us. Similarly, in some ways, it is only over time that we may be able to discern what our fathers' strongest points were, particularly in terms of their influence over us. Once years have passed, we may be able to see where their guidance was intelligent and considerate of our personalities. And thus when we return to something from our past, perhaps to paths that our fathers had mapped out for us, we do so with the knowledge that our choices have been more freely made.

As she begins her second year of graduate studies in creative writing, for example, Lita finds herself reconsidering the career in law that she had abandoned soon after her father's death. "It seems realistically to make sense for me to continue being a law professor," she says, having joined her fellow writing students as a low-paid graduate assistant for two semesters, "to have this experience behind me and go back to being a law professor and write on the side."

The decision to explore writing was extremely freeing for Lita; at forty she finally tried her hand at a childhood dream. But the reality of the writing life, one of comparative poverty or of teaching, has shown her the value of her former tenured position. The writing is part of her now, and she intends to complete her master's degree by next year. But she has begun to consider other law school jobs, as well. After some time away, she values the relative prosperity of a legal scholar, and she can appreciate the value of her education and skill in that highly specialized field. When law was something that her father had insisted upon, it had less value. Now that she can see herself as a smart and scholarly lawyer, an independent woman, she feels more at ease using this skill to support herself, even if her legal work simply serves to finance her career as an aspiring novelist.

"It really still feels like grad school has been an opportunity of a lifetime," she says. "Not every moment has been a pure joy, but my writing is better. And I'm doing it, whereas I wasn't doing it before. By the end of the third year, I will have produced a book-length manuscript, which I would never have done otherwise. And I would have been miserable with myself because I didn't. So I absolutely had to do this." For Lita, the journey may have proved to be a detour, but that does not diminish its value in her life.

For me, the journey has wound through every aspect of my life; it has touched my heart and my sense of myself. It has changed my approach to life, and thus my life itself. In terms of my dating and mating habits, I look back and see how my winter of heartlessness led to the spring wedding Jon and I would celebrate a few years later. Perhaps because of the way my father had dominated my life, had defined so tightly what a man is or what he should be to a woman, I needed to detach from my own romantic longings before I could actually bond with someone. In terms of my life's work, it took longer. Perhaps I needed to prove that I could be as responsible as my father desired. More likely, it simply took a few more years before I could see that I was ready to incorporate the lessons of security and sense that he had taught me into a career of my own making. In terms of my relationship with my mother, it has been humbling and gratifying, in turns. We still squabble, we probably always will, but if I am now better able to see her as a woman, as an adult separate from myself, then perhaps this trauma has helped prepare me for the inevitable next stage, when I will be caring for her as she grows older.

For me, the past eight years have been an excursion into a wilderness full of freedom and rage. Now that I have returned to what feels like a safe and stable place, I can look around me at the home I have made, at my marriage and career and the odds and ends of friendships and hobbies and habits that have come to define me, and I can enjoy them. These parts of my life are not simply inheritances any more. These are the pieces of me that have withstood trials, the parts of my heart and my soul that I have carried with me into the wilderness and brought back to build into a home.

Postscript

Last night I did something that I have feared doing for almost eight years. Last night, I took an ordinary cassette tape out of a case that I had buried underneath all the stray or mismatched earrings in my jewelry box and put it in the little cassette player that I use for interviews. And last night I heard my father's voice for the first time in almost eight years.

"I knew three grandparents," he begins, in answer to my question about the oldest relatives he remembered. *"My mother's father was dead before I was born. I knew much more about my mother's mother, because we lived in the same house, a two-family house. She was Viennese, or at least Austrian, and proud not to be Polish or Russian. She was a neat woman, very well organized, who ran a tight show and brought up her children very properly. . . ."*

The voice I heard at first made me worry that the tape was damaged. The voice I heard was lower and slower than I remembered, and I checked the speed, toying with it until my own voice came back with another question and I realized that the spooling plastic was undamaged, and that the sound transference was as accurate as a small machine allowed. What I was hearing was not the voice of the father I remembered, either jolly and boisterous or sternly authoritative. It was his last voice, slurred from drugs and pain, and I realized that what all the grief books say is, in some sense, true. I had forgotten that sound, the sound of my father dying, slower than in his prime, stumbling and stubbornly persistent, telling a nonstop narrative of a family for the most part gone.

> *"The first real recollection I have is when we were still on Fifty-second Street. My father was lighting off July Fourth firecrackers. I think that was the year Lindbergh flew, so it was 1927. I was five years old. My father lit the firecrackers—brrrrr!* (he mimics the sound of a spinning sparkler) *on the bannister, on the cement wall, and that was the year I wore the Al Smith pin. And was chastised for it. . . . "*

The stories he was telling, answering my questions about his history and that of all his family, were coming out in a steady stream, a determined monologue that served, I think, not so much to set the record straight as to carry him back, for the hour or so we sat there, to his childhood, to the two-family house he shared with his parents and aunts and uncles and Grandma Protter. Listening brought me back to that afternoon in my parents' apartment, as he reclined under a blanket with his feet up, and I sat close by to catch the flow of words that I did not dare to interrupt.

Because I did not dare, I worried from the start about the tape. I paid myself for my project in anticipatory regret. Because for years after I warned myself that the experience of the taping might be the best memory, that because of my haphazard technique, my failure to check the batteries or even the movement of the tape, these stories might be lost. That Great Aunt Tessie's improvident marriage to an Irishman would not be recorded, that her husband's enthusiastic endorsement of my mother as "a live one" and my Viennese great-grandmother's starched disapproval would be sacrificed to my poor preparations and the limitations of technology.

For years, too, I had been afraid to play this tape out of a kind of superstitious dread. Afraid that playing back that afternoon would nullify it, as if my father's recorded voice were a finite resource, one I could use up or destroy by listening, as if the little cassette were one of those early wax discs, too delicate to survive repeated use. This was all I had left, and to some extent I wanted to save it, shore it up against some bad time to come.

For whatever reason, likely the finishing of this project, the time had come. I rewound a little, to the bit about Tessie and Frank, about Marcie and Ben who had ran off to France, and Zoe, with her turbans, who became an interior decorator and—against all family traditions—a Republican.

> *"The upstairs apartment had a corner room, a little room over the staircase, and it was very well stocked with books. I remember Voltaire. It was all Ben's naturally. . . . I don't remember anyone else ever going into it. I remember seeing the first glimpse of a creative mind in the marginalia of his books, a little doodling he had done in the subway. . . ."*

That's my father, I told Jon that evening. I'd picked him up from work with the little cassette player running beside me in the car, unable to put it down. That's what he really sounded like. There, I said, rewinding to a section where my father had sounded a little livelier, his voice perking up as he described his parents arguing after a visit to his father's folks—uneducated, Polish—or his own joy in browsing their tailor shop, with its giant clothes press. Removed from the slow erosion that had somewhat camouflaged his decay while it was happening, Jon might think that the deep and deeply labored delivery that dominated the recording was the man I remembered, the man who had passed along his love of books and the sea. I wanted him to hear my father's true voice.

> *"At Public School 208, I was reasonably happy. I had some close friends, I remember them very well. We built sailboats together. I would get the masts out of my father's hangers, and we would get cheese boxes. And we would walk over the barrens to Canarsie, to an inlet, where you would see the sewage pouring out raw. We would be waylaid by the Italians. They were the only ones who lived there. It was no-man's land, but we had to sail those boats. . . ."*

As we listened, however, a different comparison became clear, not the one between my father remembered and the tape's reality. Here was Jon, the man I chose to have in my life, quietly attentive at my side as he struggled to make out the voice beneath the tape hiss and the noise of traffic. Here was the man I had chosen, holding my hand after a long day of work and listening, because it comforted me, to a history of which he had been given only the briefest of outlines before. And there was my father, rambling on.

My father was ill; listening to that tape now I can hear that he was much closer to death than I knew at the time, or than I was willing to admit. But he was my father still. There was a pride in his voice, even in the way he would correct himself, eager to be fair and to be accurate no matter what the cost. And just as characteristic as his jokes and his sense of history, so too was the gravity of a paterfamilias.

> *"And then when we moved further into the heart of Brooklyn I gave up the sailboats and I went into private school. I had a bedroom of my own, but I was separated from my crowd by the private school. I was never completely at home. It was like, what's that drama with the servants?* Upstairs, Downstairs. *There were others, more ordinary people. There were a few Jewish kids, but I had no profound attach-*

ment to the school because I didn't have friends there. But I did my work. . . ."

My father was once again setting himself up as the voice of record, the authority. He would have the final say, and a habit of a lifetime coincided, for the last time, with reality, for who else would speak of such things, once he was gone? In the forcefulness of his monologue, which barely paused as I asked for clarification, and never needed prompting, I remembered why I had caused myself such worry, why I had not paused to check that my tiny machine was capturing such priceless oral history. In his haste, in his desire to set the facts down, my father—my careful and detail-minded father, the amateur radio operator who built his first sets from scratch and who not that many years before had wired my apartment for sound—wouldn't wait for me to check on the most basic settings, couldn't stop when I motioned to him, fearing that my battery light had dimmed and gone out. Under the bluster, the intellectual rigor, was the fear of a man facing the unknown. For ninety minutes, he thought he could evade the future by retreating into the past with all the vigor he had left. And I was the daughter who didn't want to stop him, couldn't bring myself to take this last comfort away for the thirty or forty seconds it would have taken to check those levels or change those batteries.

"I had a little sailboat at that time, I had my first sailboat. It was a wooden sailboat, and we had it at, what was that town?" My father had gotten up to his courtship of my mother, when he had finished medical school and was waiting to be called up for army duty. *"All we would do was go out in that sailboat. We explored a little bit of Long Island, we went out exploring. We had a lot of fun. Until that time, I had been going with a woman who was Upper West Side, who played the piano, who gave me as a present, a token of her esteem, a picture of Brahms. She was a little too chubby for me. But she had been in the library at P&S*—Columbia Physicians and Surgeons, ("Picking up medical students," my mother

notes in the background). *And she had found out I wasn't going to see her anymore. And her mother called my mother up, and I had never seen my mother quite so quiet.*" He chuckles, and the tape ends.

Listening to the tape now, I wonder if in some way we both succeeded. Not in the way we hoped in our most inchoate wishes, perhaps, but in an afternoon lost in the past, in the love I was able to demonstrate under the shadow of loss, and in the ardor he showed for the truth, and for his family, that kept him talking in the face of death. Listening to that tape, to all of it, I can tell Jon or anyone else who is listening, "That was my father." For once, I hear the man entire.

Acknowledgments

It is a cliché to begin one's acknowledgments by saying such a personal work as this could not have been possible without the help of others. However, in this case it is true. I never would have realized the universality of my own experience were it not for the women who shared theirs with me. And I never could have written this book if these women, first my friends and then the dozens of volunteers, hadn't been candid and generous with their memories. I have kept them all anonymous to protect their privacy and that of their families, but I remember them well. Thank you.

Next up must be all the professionals—psychologists, therapists, doctors, and social workers—who not only shared their writings but took the time through interviews and e-mail to explain what they had learned. I am sure I will forget some people and mess up others' titles, and I apologize in advance, but let me at least express my deep gratitude to Thelma Jean Goodrich, director of behavioral science in the family residency training program, University of Texas-Houston Medical School; Joan Laird, professor emerita, Smith College School of Social Work; Froma Walsh, professor in the School of Social Service Administration and the Department of Psychiatry, Pritzker School of Medicine, University of Chicago; family therapist Terry Hargrave; psychotherapist Michele Bograd; Pauline Boss, professor of family social science, University of Minnesota; Charlotte J. Patterson, professor of psychology, University of Virginia; Barbara Gilfoyle, director of bereavement services for Calvary Hospital, New York; Carol Tosone, associate professor of social work, New York University; Faith Ferguson, senior research fellow, Center on Work and Family, Boston University School of Social Work; Robert D. Plotnick, professor of public affairs and social work, University of Washington; Joe Kelly of Dads and Daughters; Wade Horn of the National Fatherhood Initiative; scholars such as Frances Turnbull and fellow authors Joan Jacobs Brumberg, Patricia Reis, Esther Wachs Book, and Carmel Bird. Also incredibly helpful to me during the long hours of research were the staff of the Cambridge Public Library and Rosalie Prosser and her amazing crew at Alice Darling Secretarial Services. Thanks as well to those other consummate professionals—Tom Miller, my editor at Wiley; copy editor Miriam V. Sarzin; and Jonathan Matson of the Harold Matson Agency—for believing in my work and making this book possible.

On the homefront, nothing helps an author like a supportive crew of family and friends, especially those who know when to read and say nothing and when to read and comment on everything. For such invaluable aid I thank Chris Mesarch, Brett Milano, and Anne Trumbore. Vicki Croke, Debbie Jacobs, Louise Corrigan, and Penny Raynor all shared their confidence with me that I should indeed focus on this project, and Ann Porter helped me grow to the point where I could tackle it. My mother, Iris Simon, has been very brave and unfailingly generous in sharing her memories and providing unconditional encouragement. And my husband, Jon Garelick, has provided the love and support that has made this, as well as so much more, possible.

Recommended Reading

These books are the some of the most accessible for general readers who wish to explore further.

Akner, Lois. *How to Survive the Loss of a Parent: A Guide for Adults.* New York: Quill, 1994.

Bank, Melissa. *The Girl's Guide to Hunting and Fishing.* New York: Viking, 1999.

Benjamin, Jessica. *Bonds of Love: Psychoanalysis, Feminism, and the Problem of Domination.* New York: Pantheon Books, 1988.

———. *Like Subjects, Love Objects: Essays on Recognition and Sexual Difference.* New Haven, Conn.: Yale University Press, 1995.

Book, Esther Wachs. *Why the Best Man for the Job Is a Woman.* New York: Harper Business, 2000.

Boss, Pauline. *Ambiguous Loss: Learning to Live with Unresolved Grief.* Cambridge, Mass.: Harvard University Press, 1999.

Brumberg, Joan Jacobs. *The Body Project: An Intimate History of American Girls.* New York: Random House, 1997.

Gilligan, Carol. *In A Different Voice: Psychological Theory and Women's Development.* Cambridge, Mass.: Harvard University Press, 1993.

Kast, Verena. *Father-Daughter, Mother-Son: Freeing Ourselves from the Complexes that Bind Us.* Rockport, Mass: Element, 1997.

Kubler-Ross, Elisabeth. *On Death and Dying.* New York: Collier, 1993.

Leonard, Linda Schierse. *The Wounded Woman: Healing the Father-Daughter Relationship.* Boston; Shambhala, 1998.

Murdock, Maureen. *Fathers' Daughters: Transforming the Father-Daughter Relationship.* New York: Fawcett/Columbine, 1994.

Myers, Edward. *When Parents Die: A Guide for Adults* (revised edition). New York: Penguin Books, 1997.

Pincus, Lily. *Death and the Family: The Importance of Mourning.* New York: Vintage Books, 1976.

Reis, Patricia. *Daughters of Saturn: From Father's Daughter to Creative Woman.* New York: Continuum, 1995.

Rubin, Lillian B. *Tangled Lives: Daughters, Mothers, and the Crucible of Aging.* Boston: Beacon Press, 2000.

Wakerman, Elyce. *Father Loss: Daughters Discuss the Man Who Got Away.* New York: Henry Holt, 1987.

Bibliography

Akner, Lois. *How to Survive the Loss of a Parent: A Guide for Adults*. New York: Quill, 1994.

Appleton, William S. *Fathers and Daughters: A Father's Powerful Influence on a Woman's Life*. New York: Doubleday, 1981.

Bank, Melissa. *The Girl's Guide to Hunting and Fishing*. New York: Viking, 1999.

Barnett, Rosalind, Nazli Kibria, Grace K. Baruch, and Joseph Pleck. "Adult Daughter-Parent Relationships and Their Associations with Daughters' Subjective Well-Being and Psychological Distress." *Journal of Marriage and the Family*, v. 53, no. 1, Feb. 1991, p. 29 (14).

Benjamin, Jessica. *Bonds of Love: Psychoanalysis, Feminism, and the Problem of Domination*. New York: Pantheon Books, 1988.

———. *Like Subjects, Love Objects: Essays on Recognition and Sexual Difference*. New Haven, Conn.: Yale University Press, 1995.

Biller, Henry B. *Fathers and Families: Paternal Factors in Child Development*. Westport. Conn.: Auburn House, 1993.

Bird, Carmel, editor. *Daughters and Fathers*. Queensland, Australia: University of Queensland Press, 1997.

Bograd, Michele, and Kathy Weingarten, editors. *Reflections on Feminist Family Therapy Training*. New York: Haworth Press, 1996.

Book, Esther Wachs. *Why the Best Man for the Job Is a Woman*. New York: Harper Business, 2000.

Boss, Pauline. *Ambiguous Loss: Learning to Live with Unresolved Grief*. Cambridge, Mass.: Harvard University Press, 1999.

Bowlby, John. *Attachment* (second edition). New York: Basic Books, 1969.

Brumberg, Joan Jacobs. *The Body Project: An Intimate History of American Girls*. New York: Random House, 1997.

Chodorow, Nancy J. *The Power of Feelings: Personal Meaning in Psychoanalysis, Gender, and Culture*. New Haven, Conn.: Yale University Press, 1999.

Erickson, Beth M., Ph.D. *Longing for Dad: Father Loss and Its Impact.* Deerfield Beach, Fla.: Health Communications Inc., 1998.

Erikson, Erik H. *Identity and the Life Cycle.* New York: W.W. Norton, 1980.

Ferguson, Faith. "Kinkeepers and Gatekeepers: Kinship and Family Identity Among Single Mothers by Choice." Doctoral dissertation presented to Brandeis University, May 1999.

Fields, Suzanne. *Like Father, Like Daughter: How Father Shapes the Woman His Daughter Becomes.* Boston: Little, Brown, 1983.

Gilligan, Carol. *In A Different Voice: Psychological Theory and Women's Development.* Cambridge, Mass.: Harvard University Press, 1993.

Goodrich, Thelma Jean, editor. *Women and Power: Perspectives for Family Therapy.* New York: W. W. Norton, 1991.

Hargrave, Terry D., and Suzanne M. Hanna, editors. *The Aging Family: New Visions in Theory, Practice, and Reality.* Philadelphia: Brunner Mazel, 1997.

Herman, Judith Lewis. *Trauma and Recovery.* New York: Basic Books, 1992.

Hetherington, E. Mavis. "Effects of Father Absence on Personality Development in Adolescent Daughters." *Developmental Psychology,* v. 7, n. 7, 1972, p. 313 (13).

Horn, Wade F., editor. *Father Facts* (third edition). Gaithersburg, MD: The National Fatherhood Initiative, 1998.

Kast, Verena. *Father-Daughter, Mother-Son: Freeing Ourselves from the Complexes that Bind Us.* Rockport, Mass: Element, 1997.

Kubler-Ross, Elisabeth. *On Death and Dying.* New York: Collier, 1993.

Lamb, Michael E., editor. *The Role of the Father in Child Development* (second edition). New York: John Wiley and Sons, 1981.

———. *Nontraditional Families: Parenting and Child Development.* Hillsdale, N.J.: Lawrence Erlbaum Associates, 1982.

Leonard, Linda Schierse. *The Wounded Woman: Healing the Father-Daughter Relationship.* Boston: Shambhala, 1998.

Lerner, Harriet Goldhor. *The Dance of Anger: A Woman's Guide to Changing the Patterns of Intimate Relationships.* New York: Harper & Row, 1985.

Lyon, Joanne B., and Brian R. Vandenberg. "Father Death, Family Relationships, and Subsequent Psychological Functioning in Women." *Journal of Clinical Child Psychology,* v. 18, n. 4, Dec. 1989, p. 327 (9).

Maxted, Anna. *Getting Over It.* New York: ReganBooks, 2000.

McGinn, Daniel, and Julie Edelson Halpert. "Final Farewells." *Newsweek.* Dec. 14, 1998, pp. 60–62.

Miller, Alice. *The Drama of the Gifted Child: How Narcissistic Parents Form and Deform the Emotional Lives of Their Talented Children.* New York: Basic Books, 1981.

Murdock, Maureen. *Fathers' Daughters: Transforming the Father-Daughter Relationship.* New York: Fawcett/Columbine, 1994.

Myers, Edward. *When Parents Die: A Guide for Adults* (revised edition). New York: Penguin Books, 1997.

Patterson, Charlotte J., and Anthony R. D'Augelli, editors. *Lesbian, Gay, and Bisexual Identities in Families.* New York: Oxford University Press, 1998.

Pincus, Lily. *Death and the Family: The Importance of Mourning.* New York: Vintage, 1976.

Popenoe, David. *Life Without Father.* Cambridge, Mass.: Harvard University Press, 1996.

Reis, Patricia. *Daughters of Saturn: From Father's Daughter to Creative Woman.* New York: Continuum, 1995.

Rubin, Lillian B. *Tangled Lives: Daughters, Mothers, and the Crucible of Aging.* Boston: Beacon Press, 2000.

Secunda, Victoria. *Women and Their Fathers: The Sexual and Romantic Impact of the First Man in Your Life.* New York: Delacorte, 1992.

———. *Losing Your Parents, Finding Your Self: The Defining Turning Point of Adult Life.* New York: Hyperion, 2000.

Simon, Clea. *Mad House: Growing Up in the Shadow of Mentally Ill Siblings.* New York: Doubleday, 1997.

Turnbull, Frances L. "Childhood Bereavement and Its Long-Term Sequelae: A Phenomenological Investigation of Adjustment to Early Parent Death." Doctoral dissertation presented to Boston University School of Education: 1991.

Wakerman, Elyce. *Father Loss: Daughters Discuss the Man Who Got Away.* New York: Henry Holt, 1987.

Walsh, Froma, and Monica McGoldrick, editors. *Living Beyond Loss: Death in the Family.* New York: W. W. Norton, 1995.

Wexler, Natalie. "Of Human Bonding," *Washington Post Sunday Magazine.* Washington, D.C., June 8, 1997, p. 26 (7).

Woititz, Janet Geringer. *Adult Children of Alcoholics.* Deerfield Beach, Fla.: Health Communications Inc., 1983.

Index